Take Off The Cape, Sis!

CARING FOR THE LEADHER WITHIN

PRESENTED BY
SHAQUAN HOKE

Book Cover, Interior Book Design & Formatting: TamikaINK.com

Published By: Tamika INK

Library of Congress Cataloging – in- Publication Data has been applied for.

ISBN: 9798443149745

PRINTED IN THE UNITED STATES OF AMERICA.

Acknowledgements

This book is dedicated to all of the Caregivers, Leadhers, and nurturers. To people in my life who believed and supported me, my business endeavors and family.

To my parents, especially Sandra Smiley and Spiritual mother Sister Judy Williams for teaching me about God, Faith and prayer; thank you for fighting for me & covering me.

Thank you God for giving me the vision to serve with the gifts of creativity and compassion for humanity.

Table of Contents

Foreword By
Dr. Kishma George

In 2017, Shaquan Hoke was introduced to me through another business partner. She stated that God gave her a vision to help his people through a charity project which she named, The Courage To Give Project. Although I have been connected to some awesome women in ministry, business, and personal life I felt blessed to connect with this extraordinary person. Shaquan is so humble, soft-spoken with a quiet strength that has the power to attract and hold your attention as she commands the space that she walks in. Get to know Shaquan Hoke. It is an honor and blessing to know someone who is selfless and sweet-spirited.

Shaquan Hoke faced herculean challenges of pain and despair but she continue to persevere. She has shared her truth of being homeless with five children but never lost sight of the vision to continue to empower women to slay the Goliaths in their lives by using the power of prayer. She coupled tailored strategies by adding a plan of action and then showed women around the world how to execute the plan. Her ability to be vulnerable and share intimate periods of her journey has allowed her to heal, forgive and push past her circumstances. She relies on her faith in God, continues to be an advocate for women and families that are homeless. Her gift to this world is her incredible strength to rise above adversity while mentoring women around the world to be victorious.

1

Shaquan is featured this year on K.I.S.H. Billboard located in North Carolina, Delaware, and London. Also K.I.S.H. Magazine in January's 2022 Top 10 National Influencers issue. She has also been featured in the New York Times, and various podcasts, television, magazines, and other media. Shaquan is a Visionary, speaker, trainer, coach and now takes on a journey to care for the leadher within, "Take The Cape Off Sis" These thought-provoking intimate stories from all the amazing women in Shaquan's anthology will be an inspiration to the world.

DR. KISHMA GEORGE
CEO of K.I.S.H. Magazine
www.kish-maagzine.com

Power Within Her
By Shaquan Hoke

As a Coach in Career, Personal Development, and helping women monetize their gifts I have helped thousands of women in the span of twenty years. From facilitating workshops, creating curriculum, developing relationships with employers landing accounts to speaking on various mediums radio, television, virtual and live events. I knew how to show up and get the job done. It took me a long time to get to this space that I am in today. So, while I learned how to show up for everyone I held a secret. I failed over and over again to show up for the main person who needed help the most...I failed to show up for me.

Everyone would always compliment me on how well I had presented. There was a method to the way I would show up for each event. Image...I had to be sure to project the image that wouldn't intimidate or seem too overbearing. The goal for me was to connect to my audience so that they could look beyond the status that they believed I had and to see the woman in front of them. I wanted my potential clients to see that I was right where they are right now. That I, too, was tired of being used up to the bone and tossed aside like day-old Italian bread when someone more compliant came along. After all, being the goose that lays the golden eggs does not work if she can't be controlled.

"I need to save as many people as I can." This is what I thought to myself as I finally tasted what it felt like to be free. To have some control over my time and not have a job telling me when I could take a vacation. When I needed to go to the doctor, I finally know what it feels like to be able to schedule my appointments around the work I do from the comfort of my home. How did I learn this? It was through the gifts that I have from school, work, and my natural, God-given abilities. At a young age, I created art and sold it, wrote stories and poetry, and helped anyone who asked. Even if it would be at my own expense.

Although I now can do more creative projects, this was not always the case. For years, I have worked with various populations such as school-aged youth, young adults, veterans, seniors, and the homeless. I love working with children and youth as they love to learn and know when you care. The veterans were challenging, I learned from the seniors and veterans that were homeless. No matter what position I held I saw the clients as people. Over time working for many organizations I learned that I was limited in the way that I could help them. The organizations were more concerned about the numbers while I was concerned about helping them to attain a living wage, housing, and support services. The weight of hearing the challenges that were beyond my ability to serve them grew heavily on my shoulders. While I was praised for going above my position, I was also told I was being insubordinate. I guess I asked too many questions and thought about ways to improve the company too much.

For years I went through this revolving cycle of trying to fit into the employment world. Each time it took a toll on my health and I began to soothe myself with food that comforted me. At one of the places I worked, I was over two departments and had a stroke on the job. As a result, I was in the hospital for almost three weeks and was told I was at high risk of having a massive stroke if I did not lower the stress levels in my life...I was in my late thirties at that time. Fast forward I created Beyond A J.O.B. Inc in 2015 as I grew tired of not being able to serve to my full potential. In 2017 I created The Courage To Give Project found on Beyondajob.net where I campaign for the summer and winter to raise funds and give out career/personal development services along with personal care packages to homeless and at-risk women and their families.

I knew I was capable of doing so much more and grew tired of waiting for someone to compensate me for the work I created and produced. My first client needed coaching and a resume. I was now in business but there was something I kept putting off. My mind kept telling me something I kept forgetting. Oh, it's ok, I'll wait until... BOOM! In the passenger seat, I was in a car accident. The right side of my body and two disks in my spine were affected. Oh, the thing I kept forgetting was now screaming at me. I was supposed to go to the doctor and see about my mental and physical health. 2019 is now ending and I hear music and dancing as the ball drops to ring in 2020. Although in pain I was thankful to be able to stand and walk, even though it was very little. I know there were more surgeries and doctor's appointments in-store. I prayed, "God, please help me. This pain, I don't know how I'm going to function like this."

I had to get surgery on my right shoulder. A robotic arm was my aid in regaining mobility and flexibility. Over time I got a bit stronger but when it rains it kindly reminds me of all the injuries I've sustained. March of 2020, I was about to celebrate my born date but the news of COVID reminded me that it was praying time. The world was in turmoil and people were hurting, sick, and experiencing great loss. Daily I'd hear the ambulance drive by with blaring sirens ten to fifteen times a day. The daily death toll climbed to six hundred, my heart hurt for the nation and all I could do was pray. Then it knocked on my door. I had all of the symptoms including shortness of breath, coughing, loss of smell/taste, and fever for about ten days. The weakness and heart palpitations weeks after reminded me I must take care of myself.

I tried so hard to get back to "normal" not realizing that life for me was never really normal. Many days it was so hard to get up out of bed, shower, dress, and go outside to go anywhere. So, I would just get up. Or lay in bed and pray for the strength to rise out of the dark place I found myself in. Sleepless nights increased and my weight ballooned since the accident and have limited mobility. What was happening to me? I smiled on the outside but screamed for help on the inside, I was trapped in my own mind. I needed help so I found the courage to call the doctor and speak to a therapist. I was diagnosed with PTSD, Generalized Anxiety Disorder, and Depression. Wow! In my mid-forties, I learned the explanation to many challenges I struggled with. Walking with a cane and limited mobility did not help my self-esteem either.

It was easy for me to focus on someone who needed my help. In fact, it was a welcomed distraction that made me feel like I was worthy to be alive. Now that I have the answer to behaviors, I struggled with I now knew what to go to God in prayer. According to the doctors, I should be on several medications to function and to sleep. Although meds were prescribed, I knew that was not how I wanted to live my life. So I asked God to provide the knowledge and resources to treat myself naturally. I wanted to be healed and learn to cope with triggers as they arise. Through prayer, I discovered I had to face the past traumas of sexual abuse as a child, homelessness, physical abuse, divorce, and abandonment from people I loved. I just went through life on autopilot. My children are my world and they were all I fought for. I never really fought for myself. So the patterns of me saving everyone around me was a way to save a part of myself. I saw me in them. Now I can see it was me that I was saving all the time.

Through the years I learned that no one was coming to save me or my children. There was no knight in shining armor to slay the evil that was trying to consume me. The flesh is just what it is and it seeks comfort, pleasure, and self-preservation. The power I looked for was already inside of me. Although I was triggered and have had to struggle my way through the dark times I never gave up. My God that spoke to the debts of my inner being showed me the light that was hidden. It was buried beneath all the trauma, through the past disappointments, anger, and pain.

The one thing that held me together was the power of praying the word of God. The knowledge that whatever I needed was somewhere deep inside of me and I could activate the strength I needed wherever I was. Knowing that although many times I felt so alone and in pain I was never alone. God was always with me and at times carried me when I could not bear to stand.

Psalm 23 (A Psalm of David.)

1 The LORD is my shepherd; I shall not want.
2 He maketh me to lie down in green pastures: he leadeth me beside the still waters.
3 He resorteh my soul: he leadeth me in the paths of righteousness for his name's sake.
4 Yea, though I walk through the valley of the shadow of death, I will fear no evil: for thou art with me; thy rod and thy staff they comfort me.
5 Thou preparest a table before me in the presence of mine enemies: thou anointest my head with oil; my cup runneth over.
6 Surely goodness and mercy shall follow me all the days of my life: and I will dwell in the house of the LORD forever.

About the Visionary
Shaquan Hoke

Shaquan Hoke, Founder, and C.E.O. of **Beyond A J.O.B. Inc.**, The Courage To Give Project, and recently founded **Loc N Love L.L.C.** – Beyond A Job offers Career and Job Readiness Services, is a three-time Amazon Best Selling Author, Inspirational Speaker, and Trainer with over ten years of Professional Business Experience, Recruitment, Development, Sales and Job Readiness. Her company assists in attaining the tools needed to gain employment or map out a professional career, personal and business leadership coaching, inspirational speaking, and leadership training to organizations worldwide. Shaquan's focus is on the quality of service provided, not the quantity of clients served. She views her clients as dynamic and diverse individuals who have ever-changing life demands and evolving goals. No matter your aspirations, Shaquan believes you can address your personal goals with a customized plan tailored for your success.

Shaquan completed her first solo book in 2017, "The Audacity To Rise: Seven Steps to Create & Move Into Your Vision," which details her transition to true freedom through the application of Prayer. On May 6, 2021, she lead and published her first Anthology, "Rising Crowns of Glory". She also has a Planner for Job and Opportunity Seekers who want to stay organized. Additional anthologies authored are found on Amazon, Barnes & Nobles, and at www.beyondajob.net

A humanitarian and spiritual believer in Christ, she spearheaded the **Courage to Give Project** in 2017, which Annually serves over 200 homeless and low-income women and female veterans with Personal Care Packages. Shaquan was featured in New York Times Magazine 2/2020, Refinery 29, Bronx Net News T.V., and mentioned on NY1, C.B.S. 2, and N.B.C. 4 in her efforts to help the homeless. She has been featured in D.S.E. magazine, Boss Magazine, Kish Magazine, contributing writer to the new iWorshop96 Magazine, and an Influencer/Content Creator for Women on the Rise Network. A highly sought-after Speaker on Job Readiness and Personal Development Coach in her local community and across the United States.

Shaquan has facilitated workshops, professional training and is an Associate Professional Women's Group Member at Dress for Success World Wide. She conducted professional training at Microsoft, Bronx

Community College, Easter Seals NY, New York Urban League, and many others. Beyond A Job has proven success strategies and methodologies for career and employment services, effective communication, critical thinking, and understanding behaviors that support and maintain healthy relationships.

Shaquan walks in her divine purpose daily as a servant and leader to empower others to become the best person that they can be and ultimately fulfill their divine destiny in life. For additional information, visit the website or email support@beyondajob.net

The Power of Prayer
By Sis. Judy Williams

S is. Judy Williams married the late Elder Asher Williams and raised a daughter and two of her nieces. She is affectionately known as a spiritual mother due to her love and dedication to the women whose lives she has touched. Sister Judy Williams was given a position to lead the Pentecostal Church of God aka PCG over district two Women's Department which comprised several churches on the northern end. She took great pride to lead by example in teaching women how to pray, conduct themselves as a godly woman, how to manage a house as a wife, motherhood, and many other areas, both natural and spiritual. Although many people came to her for help and advice, she always directed them in the ways of the Lord, careful to ensure her instruction was approved by leadership of the local Pastor and Bishop over District two. In addition to mentoring the women's department, her heart was really with the youth. Sis. Williams saw the pressures that the young people of today had, and she created a safe space for them to express themselves. At least twice a month, Sis. Judy Williams would take the young girls, she called them, her "little people" to her home economics, family issues, school, prayer, etc. It became an open forum for the little people to express themselves and in turn, they would be mentored in the ways of the Lord in both natural and spiritual matters. She enjoyed taking time with the youth as they still come to her for advice to this day. When she first started this, she created a booklet that demonstrated all of the activities she did with them such as cooking, sewing, etc.

In Corporate America, Judy worked as an accountant for Marsel Mirror and Glass for over twenty years. Once she transitioned from Marsel, she prayed for a specific type of job that would work for her. God answered her prayers and opened the position for her to work as an accountant for the American Red Cross for about seven years until she began to get ill. Once again the Lord opened up a door where she received disability social security in three months which was very unusual.

Judy Williams was introduced to PCG through her husband, Elder Asher Williams, where he was a pastor for thirty years. This meant for her to wear many hats as the pastor's wife. She previously belonged to another faith and was skeptical due to having a bad experience. When you have been burned by a blue match and now you are introduced to a red match, the thought is you will still get burned. It was not easy for her, in the beginning, to view the church through the lenses of painful eyes. However, when she heard the man of God preaching the gospel, she knew in her heart that she was finally in the right place. She could not imagine being anywhere else as her soul was fed the bread of life. There was no other place she'd rather be than to be in the house of the Lord. To this day, she has been a servant in PCG for forty-two years.

When asked what her favorite scripture to refer to when times are tough, she stated that she did not have a favorite scripture. She used prayer as her weapon of choice when times were tough. In her exact words, "Many times we pray to God for help, but when the prayer is over we pick it back up instead of surrendering it over. I've learned not to hold on but to let go and let God. He has never failed or left me...even though I left him so many times."

You must have faith when you pray that God will hear and answer you. God already knows what we need, and all you have to do sometimes is just ask. Sister Judy Williams, although she is no longer over the

Women's Department of district two, is and will always be a servant leader and prayer woman. Judy always had plans a, b, c or d and one of them always worked. But when you find your back against the wall and start crying out to the Lord in prayer, things began to move. That's when you know it was nothing but the Lord that made a way. If I leave nothing else with you know that prayer is a weapon, and the Lord is always with you if you believe and have faith.

The Greatest Love Of All
by Andrenee Boothe

Learning to love yourself; it is the greatest love of all –
Whitney Houston

I can see you right now, holding your imaginary microphone and singing like you know the greatest love of all is happening to you right now in this very moment. As a matter of fact, I'm singing along right with you, because we are on this evolutionary journey of learning to love ourselves. This is a journey of more than 1000 miles, but if you take it, you will find joy, courage, wisdom, heartbreak, betrayal, ups, downs, confusion, clarity, and so much more. But if there is one thing that I am banking on, that would be that it is a journey worth taking. I am not sure where you are on this journey. Maybe you are at the beginning, or you are at the tail end, wherever you are, I want you to know that I am super proud of you. This journey is not for the faint at heart, but the good news is, you have gained a sister in me. Sis, we are in this together, and you are NOT alone. I am writing to you, not from a space of "I have arrived," but from a space of compassion, understanding, empathy, and most importantly love. Let's just take a moment right here and take a deep cleansing breath. You're going to find that every now and then I'm going to ask if we could just pause and take a breath together because our breath is the one thing that reminds us that we can choose again and again and again.

If you are like me, you too are a woman who wears many hats. Some of these hats look like somebody's mama, somebody's sister, somebody's star employee, somebody's go-to person, somebody's daughter, somebody's caretaker, somebody's best friend, somebody's auntie, somebody's hairdresser, somebody's wife, somebody's baby mama, somebody's grandma.....somebody's SOMEBODY. One way or another when others see you, they see a long flowing cape, and they know you are someone with a big heart, great integrity, super strength, passion, hope, grit, and resilience. Sis, You are the ONE! You got IT! There's just something about You that makes others feel like they can depend on You. When you wear that cape there is absolutely nothing you cannot do. Heck, I shock myself sometimes after accomplishing what appears to be an impossible daily feat.

I think it's a beautiful thing to be a person that cares for others and to want to make sure that the people you love are always good, but not at the expense of losing yourself. Not at the expense of everyone loving and appreciating the wonderful person that you are, yet not feeling that way towards yourself. I had no idea that wearing my cape would reveal some of the hardest truths about me. My superwoman cape became the mirror that would show me the things that I was hiding behind.

It was a Sunday evening, the last day of my church's (at the time) annual youth weekend. I was Youth Choir Director and Secretary of the Youth

Department. I was also a very avid churchgoer. Although being the single mother of an amazing pre-teen, and working late hours at a full-time job, I would be at church whenever the doors opened. I can remember always feeling the need to be at church. I felt like I owed God my all and so if I showed up and participated, then God would be pleased with me. Well, our annual youth weekend was on fire. The messages were life-changing, the choir sounded amazing and souls were giving their life back to God. We were all on a high and didn't want it to come to an end. But of course, it was the last night and our pastor gave his final remarks. My expectation of his remarks would be words of praise, particularly to those of us who worked hard at making the event a success, but the opposite happened. Words were said that shattered everything inside of me. It was as if something fired a semi-automatic straight through me. I left that event so heavy I thought I was going to die.

I can remember that week being one of the darkest weeks I experienced. In my mind, I thought, I am doing everything in my power to show how dedicated I am, yet it's just not enough. It was then I realized that nothing I could ever do will win the love and acceptance of others. That I could do everything right, be at every service, dot all of my "i's", cross all of my "t's", and still come up short in the eyes of another. I can also remember being so exhausted and burnt out. I felt depleted and as dry as a desert. I didn't want to live anymore. I was over everything and everyone. It was then I had a conversation with God, and for the first time, I actually listened.

I said to God, "I don't want to go to that church anymore. I'm tired, and I'm done. Please promise me you won't leave me. I just don't want to do this church thing, it's not working." Then I heard "I will never leave you, wherever you go, I will go". That was all I needed to hear. Those words stood with me during the scariest and most uncertain times, and they continue to stay with me. This was the beginning of what I would call my journey of self-love/self-discovery. You see, I had a lot of information about God and the Bible, but my journey of KNOWING God began when my journey of discovery MYSELF began. To know myself is to know who and what God is. This simultaneously led me to my journey of self-love.

One of the first things that I discovered was that I didn't really like myself. I did not like the woman I would look at in the mirror every day. Yes, I would comb my hair, put on makeup and dress nicely, but I hated the woman within. I thought myself as a failure. There were things I did in my past that I thought could never be forgiven. I discovered that I had very deep feelings of unworthiness for the things I had done *(if you can relate, pause right here and take a deep cleansing breath)*. This discovery led me to someone who mentored me back to my true identity. I had to relearn who I was. I thought my identity was wrapped up in the titles that I held, i.e. somebody's SOMEBODY, but who I am is an unrepeatable brilliant idea in and from the Mind of God, and nothing that I ever do can take that identity from me. I had to relearn how to see myself. I now see myself as God sees me, perfect, whole, and complete.

I then had to heal my God concept. The God that I learned about at church was a god I had to make parts with *(if you can relate, pause right here and take a deep cleansing breath)*. It had served me long enough. I had to release the idea of a god who was taking a tally of all of my rights and wrongs as well as watching if I was being naughty or nice. The god who was sitting on a rocking chair up in the sky with a white long beard became another fairytale for me. I began to embrace the idea of God being one with me. God is the everywhere-evenly presence of absolute good that can never be separate from me. God is the Spirit of Absolute Good. God is the ALL. This new way of understanding and experiencing God has revolutionized my life in ways that I cannot put into words.

Once I healed my God concept, it was easier for me to start to love the woman in the mirror. The woman in the mirror started to look more and more beautiful. The scales of shame had been removed from my eyes and replaced with a lens of love. You see, I was waiting for others to see me, to acknowledge the beauty in me, to validate my worthiness, and to accept me with all of my mistakes. Little did I know that I was the one that I had been waiting for. The cape was a cover. It was what I used to hide behind until I couldn't hide anymore. It took the feeling of wanting to die for me to finally take the cape off!!

Has taking the cape off been easy? The easy part is taking it off. The hard part is keeping it off lol. Remember, this is a journey and not a race. There are times you will put it back on. There are times you will forget. There are times you want to give up, but here are some life practices that I implement daily to keep me grounded. When you find that you are losing your sense of self, it means you have stopped practicing. Life is a practice. What you practice daily becomes a habit and your habits become your character. It doesn't matter how good of a person you are, if you neglect taking care of yourself, you will deplete.

1. Learn how to say **"NO"** to what is not in alignment with your core values. Create a schedule for yourself and stick to it. Be unapologetic about your life plans. In order for you to know your core values, you have to have a relationship with yourself. Take the journey of self-discovery, I promise you it won't offend God in any way *(pause and take a breath)*.

2. Stop being "**NICE**". My mom used to say to me, we weren't called to be nice; we were called to be good people. Be authentically you. If that means some people aren't going to like you, oh well. Release the fear of people not accepting you and embrace those who love you just the way you are *(pause and take a breath)*.

3. Be **"NAKED"** and unashamed. Accept every single part of who you are because every single part of what God made of you is GOOD. Let's tear down the barriers of shame and allow what is imperfect about you to shine through. I have found that things that I find imperfect about me, others absolutely adore. No more hiding behind the cape *(pause and take a breath)*.

4. Start saying **"YES"** to your desires. Everything you desire you can have. God would not have put the desire there if you couldn't have it. You are WORTHY of everything good in this life, but you must first believe it and agree with your YES!

5. Learn to **"YIELD"** to the GODdess within. Remember earlier when I spoke about my breaking moment and me having that conversation with God. That was a YIELD moment. I paused and leaned within. I stopped looking outside of myself for the answers. That voice is always speaking to You and can I share with you a little secret? That voice sounds just like your voice. Make the time to YIELD and listen to that voice more often.

6. Leave **"YESTERDAY"** where it belongs; in the past. I think one of the hardest things for us to do is accept that there is absolutely nothing we can do to change what has already happened. We quietly live in regret and wish things were

different. I am now of the belief that if it happened, it was supposed to. No matter how bad it looks, and from that knowledge, I am able to move on. We must no longer allow the past to keep us captive. Regret is the breeding ground for condemnation and condemnation only leads us back to the addiction of needing approval from others, and then there goes that cape again. No more!!

In conclusion, I need for you to know that You are loved. Love is not something you have to work for. It isn't something you earn. It is who You are at the core. But this is information You must KNOW deep down in your soul. For years I hid behind a cape because I was afraid to face myself. I wore the cape so that I could give everyone else that responsibility. The responsibility of choosing me first. We are no good to everyone if we are no good to ourselves. If you are already on this journey, again I am super proud of you. If you are just starting, sis, I am right here cheering you on. It's going to get scary and even lonely at times, but always remember you are not alone, for God is with you always.

Matthew 28:20
"Behold, I am with you always, even to the end of age, Amen."

About
Andrenee Boothe

Andrenee Boothe, Master Life Strategist & Lifestyle Coach is the Founder and CEO of Andrenee's Corner, a Sacred Space in the World where Women's lives are enhanced with practical life strategies to help women be the best version of themselves.

To date, Andrenee has served many women with tools, resources, training, and support, establishing Andrenee as the go-to expert for women who want to do life on a higher plane and, in turn, reap higher life experiences and live the life of their dreams.

Her coaching philosophy is rooted in spiritual principles, strategic planning, inspired action, and implementation. She is also the Leader of a thriving

Facebook Community "A Tribe Called Beautiful". In this space, women are awakening to their true identity and harnessing the power that lies within to take their lives to the next dimension.

Andrenee understands that identity, individuality, and intimacy is the catalyst to a powerful and meaningful life. With her signature program, "The Beautiful You Experience", she is giving women all over the world the permission to see themselves as the Magnificent beings they truly are, and as result, manifest dreams they once thought were only imaginable.

Meet Andrenee:
at https://www.andrenee.com/home.

On the Potter's Wheel
By Andria Eanes

Love and abundant blessings to all. May the work I've done speak for me and may the love of God, His grace and mercy be with all who read, receive, and understand.

Many times in life we find ourselves on the potter's wheel. What do I mean, you may ask. Well, as far back as junior high school I remember taking a ceramics class. I was excited about learning a new craft and creating a new masterpiece whether it was a dish, a vase, or an ashtray. This class often put you to the test of how skillful you were at your craft and finishing with a beautiful and refined product.

The challenge would often come when the clay on the potter's wheel would crack, crumble or fall apart from its molten state. Although it was amazing to watch the clay spin into its purpose, there were times the mold just couldn't be fixed so I would find myself forced to bring it all the way down and start all over again.

I believe that in the circle of life we find ourselves on the potter's wheel. Ups and downs, round and round, and sometimes just a plain mess. But God has a way of respinning our wheel and lifting us into the beautiful product He wants us to be.

It's 4 AM and time to put on my uniform and go to work operating a bus for the NYC Transit Authority for 24 plus years ... up and down the roads of Queens,

NY, in all kind of weather, dealing with unstructured road conditions, and meeting various people through all walks of life.

I was grateful as I loved my job and the many people I found connections with. I was also proud and honored to follow in my father's footsteps as he worked as a conductor for Transit, taking care of his family, and retiring after 20 years of service.

Work ethic has always been very important yet not as important to me as the care and safety of my passengers, co-workers, and friends. Often felt unappreciated but our love for one another lifted us up and made it all worthwhile.

Trip sheet in! Cape off, Sis! Time to go home after a long, hard, and trying day. Grateful and blessed to have finished the task knowing I was one step closer to retirement.

Isn't it funny how we form our own plans for life, looking at the hopes and dreams of others and all that they have accomplished, praying that it will be you, just to find out later those plans weren't for you? Jeremiah 29:11.

Tired, stressed, body breaking down ... this job was becoming a bit much, besides my other full-time job as a mom, wife, family member, and friend was waiting. No time for woes, cape on! Cooking, cleaning, shopping, washing clothes, never stopping to take a moment for me or God. Weekend entertainment, chores, and family activities just made for a full, or what I thought a prosperous week. But it wasn't about me anyway, I thought.

You have a responsibility to serve ... but serve who? I found myself day in, and day out, doing the same routine. There started to become cracks in the clay and I was swiftly falling apart.

Depression, anxiety quickly took place... feeling hopeless that all life had to offer me was thrown away. Sleeping down in the basement of the home I grew up in and feeling the walls closing in on me. I didn't feel I could get up. Everything in my life seemed dead. I had lost my job, my home, my marriage, some family, and some friends. No health insurance. My money was low and my bills were due. Autoimmune disease was taking a toll on my health. I had no idea how I would make it. I needed the potter to work ... for the clay was a complete mess, and I knew I had to throw this cape away.

Where was the love and support from all those whom I loved? The ones who lifted me up when I took that drink, or, when I dropped it like it was hot. Where was the family who consistently depended on me to make things happen, but wouldn't make things happen for me? Where was the job I thought gave promise for a great future and where did I go? The love I once had for myself but not realizing the reality that I failed to love myself.

BUT GOD What does it profit a man to gain the whole wide world but to lose his soul. God was speaking to me through His spirit. Yes, even in all my mess, He said I am the potter and you are the clay. I will make you over if you will just pray, and I cried, and I prayed, and I told God I trusted Him and wanted a change. I said yes to His will and yes to His way even when the odds were against me. But He said, your gifts will make room for you and He has made me blessed to be a blessing.

Still putting on and taking those capes off, sis, and I will continue until I fly away. Thank you to God's planted angels, my beloved mom, Julia Eanes, my sister, Pamela Eanes, my two amazing daughters, Monica, and Nyah, my mentor and godsister, Cheryl Greene, my mentor and friend, Shaquan Hoke, and last but never least, my love, my confidante, Michael Minette.

Jeremiah 29:11 - *For I know the plans I have for you declared the Lord, plans to prosper you and not to harm you. Plans to give you hope and a future.*

Structured - God first, then me, then family, and all else to follow.

About
Andria D. Eanes

A ndria D. Eanes is a spiritual and inspirational thought leader who uses her gifts to powerfully guide, encourage, and motivate. She is a loving mother of two, a daughter, a sister, a friend and opens her heart to all who embrace her.

Andria is a former Bus Operator for New York Transit Authority. She also worked for NYPD as an Office Aide in the Arrest & Crime Coding Unit for ten years prior to her career at Transit. She is currently an Entrepreneur, Founder, and Business Owner of Andria's Creations. Her business services her customers by creating beautiful and tasty desserts, foods, treats, party favors, and more. Her business has allowed her to support her family and bless others who are in need, mainly in her community. Andria is determined to make a difference in someone's life, daily, one person at a time.

Andria was born in May 1968, in Brooklyn, NY. She was raised in Cambria Heights, Queens, where she has served most of her life. She has been an active member of the Allen AME Cathedral in Jamaica, NY for over forty years. She is an alumnus of Andrew Jackson High School (Class of '86), and continues to have a prominent relationship with her former AJ family.

Andria's goals are to live, love, laugh and enjoy her life to the fullest despite the circumstances she encounters. She is determined to make a difference in the lives that surround her through her spiritual journey and life's experiences. Her motto is "Blessed to be a Blessing" and to spread love's message to the world while never forgetting to love God and herself first. She is a Christian, singer, poet, spiritual encourager, and most of all a survivor of life's challenges. Andria Eanes wholeheartedly believes in the love of God, self-love, love relationships, and the love of family, friends, and the world.

CAPE of The Runners Journey
by Ciara Thomas

I am a runner by nature, no, not the track and field kind of runner. No, I mean the Habakkuk 2:2 type of runner, where the LORD tells the prophet Habakkuk to "write the vision, and make it plain upon tables, that he may "run" that read it." I'm that kind of runner or at least that is how I like to believe that I am. Especially within the church and marketplace. However, I'm sort of a Jonah when it comes to facing my insufficiencies and emotions. Jonah was an Old Testament prophet who decided to try to run from God and was swallowed by a giant fish but in the end, still had to face the very thing he was trying to run from. And though I had spent many years running from and trying to hide certain insufficiencies and emotions in the end I had to face them.

I grew up in the south side of Queens in Jamacia, NY with my aunt and her 5 out of 6 kids with 2 of my siblings in a 5-bedroom apartment in Baisley Projects. If you want to know anything about a superwoman my aunt was close to it raising 8 kids on her own. Well, actually 9 to be exact. I was never really outgoing, kind of stayed to myself, and had really one close friend, Tierra Gloria White. She lived on the 4th floor, and I lived on the 1st. We went to the same elementary and junior high school together and separated for high school. What I didn't know is that that separation would become permanent after she turned 18. I never knew we wouldn't grow old together and become each other's children's godmother. I never thought she would go so soon.

I never really knew how to deal with death, especially someone so close. So, I did what I knew how to do, what I did in the past. I convinced myself that she wasn't dead but away so that I wouldn't have to face the pain of losing my best friend. It was bad enough that I saw her there in the hospital bed laying there so peacefully. I really thought she was asleep until after standing there for a little while I realized that the machines were off, I noticed because the last time I was there for some reason that was all I paid attention to, and then the nurse rushed over and asked if I was her sister and told me she had passed. It felt so surreal, and I didn't know how to react or how to properly process what was said so I told myself repeatedly out loud while walking to and standing at the elevator, "she's not dead, she's just sleeping".

This had become one of my habits. Running from and running too. Running from the pain, hurt, emotions, responsibilities because of feelings of inadequacy and running to work, church, someone else's aid, or a false narrative. My thoughts: if it couldn't happen for me then I would do all that I could to make it happen for someone else. If I could just put all my time, effort, strength, and resources into helping somebody else make it then I will not have to face me and all that I am dealing with. If I just run and leave it all undone, I will never have to face it. But just like in Jonah's story that wasn't God's plan.

Cape Creation

So how did I get like this? It didn't start with the passing of my best friend when I was 17. No, this begin 13 years before when my 3 siblings and I returned home from school to a locked door. When our parents couldn't return home because they had been arrested and in jail for about a month according to my mom. Unknowingly my cape creation began there.

Thankfully, our neighbor was very kind and let me, my brother, and my sister stay with her while my eldest brother went to stay at his friend's house. After about two weeks or more my eldest brother called one of our aunts and she came and got us and brought us to our grandmother's house where we lived for about a year. But now with 4 extra mouths to feed it was a bit much so it was decided that we would become wards of the state through kinship and that our other aunt would take us in and raise us.

I was too young to understand it but a part of me felt kind of rejected but happy that my aunt was taking us in. I remember one day questioning myself as to why I never cried about my parents not returning for us. I remember standing in front of the double door linen closet in the hallway of our apartment and forcing myself to cry, forcing myself to miss my mother because I just thought it was so unnatural to not miss them not knowing that I had begun to build up walls.

As I got older, I had adopted the saying "everything happens for a reason." So anytime something would happen to me or trigger certain emotions I would use this saying as a coping and cover-up mechanism so that I didn't have to face certain feelings or situations. By this time, I had begun to master running from my feelings but in this process began forming nasty insecurities like unworthiness and lack of confidence.

Unveiling My Cape

When I turned 14, we were required to attend Independent Living Programming as transitional programming for aging out of foster care. I enjoyed going because it got me out of the house. Then I had seemed to always be on punishment and that meant I couldn't go anywhere so I was grateful for this program. From the beginning, it seemed to me that the Lord had placed me on the radar of the presenters though I never really spoke. Actually, I was very quiet, observant, and to myself in the back always trying to hide. But they saw something.

I remember one day after programming one of the presenters came to me and told me that she would like me to join the Peer Leadership Council because she thought that I would be a good fit. I didn't understand how. I was shy and to myself and didn't believe I had anything to offer but I agreed. Not because I saw what she did in me but to have a place of belonging and in the process if I could be a part of something that could assist someone else. I was for it.

Thus began my journey of focusing on others.

By the time I had aged out of foster care, through the Peer Leadership Council, I had received my certification in facilitation, helped brought awareness to the struggles of foster care youth through a video publication, assisted in the beginning discussions of law changes for youth aging out of foster care, facilitated and co-facilitated foster parent and youth workshops, caseworker and youth workshops, mentored children in foster care and so much more. On the outside, it looked great but, in the end, I still had to go home and face me. The unsure me, the me who still felt unworthy, the me who found love in all the wrong places. The me who still struggled to see what they saw in me. The me who was still running.

But that was all about to come to an end.

I had given my life to the LORD at the age of 22 but I began to notice His pursuit for me around 19/20. I became very involved in church. This is where I had got the whole Habakkuk runner concept from. There was a purpose, the King's purpose and I was going to be a part of it. I was involved in almost everything and I didn't really realize it until one year I wrote out everything I was involved in, one, to know the areas I needed to organize myself and two, to prepare myself mentally for what I needed to tackle or so I thought.

I split it into 3 categories "Church, Work, and Family." I wrote out every department I was a part of: first was Evangelism and Outreach because I was the head of that department, I had to plan for our 3 major events that were coming up, the evangelism & back to school community BBQ, Thanksgiving, and Christmas Outreach as well as the schedule and materials for the shelter bible study outreach and street evangelism. Next was the Children's church department because I was one of the teachers and had to prepare lessons, then there were 2 other departments that I participated in that I would have to make time for rehearsals or anything else that may be needed.

Next was the work category. Here, we were trying to create a new system for our participants so that meant creating new or revised curriculum and forms to try to fast track but effectively assess and track each participant as well as facilitate and assist participants with creating their resumes. Then there was the family category that consisted of a cleaning, cooking, and family time schedule. Here though was where I dropped the ball most of the time, which was a part of the reason, I begin looking into it all but there were still my underlined issues that I was running from, and at home was where I would have to face them.

The Struggle of Removal

I believe a week or two after creating that list I was placed on a sabbatical at church and had to text the things I was involved in for them to delegate to other members. It felt weird but now I had no choice but to focus more on home and work. I don't know why but home to me I always kind of equated to having to face the things I had been running from for so many years. I couldn't wait to get off my sabbatical, I couldn't wait to get back to it all. I was afraid of becoming too comfortable but that also meant I wasn't getting what the Lord needed me to get. I wasn't listening. I thought that by being involved I was doing the right, but I was being a Martha (Luke 10:38-42), busy trying to serve Jesus and missing what really mattered at that moment, being at Jesus' feet listening and learning from Him.

Once my sabbatical was over, I was at it again. Back on the praise and worship team, prepping for the Christmas outreach, rehearsing for the Christmas play. And once again at the beginning of the year, my friend and I came together and created our goal books for the new year and this time it was more in-depth. It still had the three main categories but also included an additional category for any personal goals we wanted to pursue that year. I even remember presenting it to the church at bible study one night. But as Proverbs 16:9 states, *"We can make our plans, but the LORD determines our steps."* and that He did.

Three months later everything shifted. I... was... devastated! Never in a million years did I think that the Lord would lead my family from the church we were in. I was hurt to my core, and it opened up every wound it took years for me to shut out. This time I couldn't run, I couldn't pretend like all was well, like there was some distant land. No, this time I had to face it. I had to face the pain, the hurt, the loneliness, the rejection. I had to face it all and go through the process that the Lord was taking me through to remove and renew what He wanted to. I had no choice but to cry, sit at His feet, listen and learn.

Taking The Cape Off

During this process, the Lord began to show me me. The insecure me, the doubting me, the fearful me, and everything else that I had been running from over the years. And it was ugly, but I was grateful. I was grateful because I knew I could face it because I wasn't alone. He was there and I could come to Him in humility and repentance with no judgment.

In the past, I didn't know him so to face those things then meant facing it alone. Sure, there were other people there, but could they have handled my mess with no judgment? Only God knows. There was a fear there, one that I held on to even after I had given my life to Christ. I would open up but only to a certain point. It was like letting Jesus into my home telling Him He was welcomed anywhere but that one dirty room in the back because I didn't know how to properly clean it and anytime I tried I felt overwhelmed. So how could I let another individual in there?

Then He begin to show me that my identity and sense of worth were too wrapped up in what I was doing for Him as opposed to who He said that I am. Which made it difficult for me to let go because I felt like I was losing who I thought I was. I had to realize and stand on the fact that I was His, His daughter, a true child of the King, and that I was worth so much to Him that He died for me, pursued me, rescued me, and made me His. He did this not because I did the right things but simply because He loves me and not just me but every one of us and because I have accepted Christ, I have complete access.

Walking Away Cape Free

So now I can face those things I ran from in the past and take them to the Lord in prayer with no shame. Now when I do anything I remind myself that this is my assignment, not my identity. My identity is found in Him and that doesn't change but the assignment can. So, what I do is not who I am it's what I've been assigned to do to fulfill His will and bring Him glory.

Lessons Through the Journey

Though there is more to my journey, I am eternally grateful for the lessons I have learned along the way thus far. Lessons that will be with me throughout the next journey of my life. Lessons I will never let go of that will continue to help me grow.

Through this journey, I have learned to:

1. **Make sure I am running with God's vision and not my own.** There is a season for everything but when the Lord is shifting things in another direction, I must be ready and willing to move with that shift or else I will continue to keep running in a direction that He isn't leading me.

2. **Never be too busy trying to serve the Lord when He is trying to get me to be still and sit at His feet so I can hear what He is saying.** Too much movement or too much activity can make me miss what God is saying. Miss the beauty of a deeper relationship with Him. So, though a thing might be right, it might not be right for me in that season. I

must be ok with that. It just means that God is doing something new in me, around me, with me, and for me so that He can do something new through me. So, in those seasons I must sit still and hear what He has to say.

3. **No more running from my insufficiencies, insecurities, and emotions.** They just remind me that I am human and how much I need the Lord. So, I must face them and run with them to Jesus because He loves taking our messes in exchange for His best. He is the same God that still gives us beauty for ashes, the oil of joy for mourning, and the garment of praise for the spirit of heaviness *(Isaiah 61:3)*.

4. **My God-given assignment is just that, my God-given assignment, and it is subject to change according to His will.** That change does not negate who I am in Christ because my identity is found in Him and who He says that I am and nothing else.

Be Encouraged

So, when we are in the midst of those moments in our journey when we may find ourselves running either to or from. Stop for a moment and listen. Listen to see if the Lord is trying to get your attention. See if He is trying to change your position. Your position from broken to whole, from death to life, from captive to set free. See if He is trying to make you, cape free.

Jesus said, *"Come unto me, all ye that labour and are heavy laden, and I will give you rest. Take my yoke upon you, and learn of me; for I am meek and lowly in heart: and ye shall find rest unto your souls. For my yoke is easy, and my burden is light."* (Matthew 11:28-30)

Scriptures That Helped Me Through My Journey

Jeremiah 29:11 *"For I know the thoughts that I think toward you, saith the LORD, thoughts of peace, and not of evil, to give you an expected end."*

Isaiah 41:10 *"Fear thou not; for I am with thee: be not dismayed; for I am thy God: I will strengthen thee; yea, I will help thee; yea, I will uphold thee with the right hand of my righteousness."*

Proverbs 28:13 *"He that covereth his sins shall not prosper: but whoso confesseth and forsaketh them shall have mercy."*

1 Peter 5:7 *"Casting all your care upon him; for he careth for you."*

Philippians 1:6 *"Being confident of this very thing, that he which hath begun a good work in you will perform it until the day of Jesus Christ:"*

About
Ciara Thomas

C iara Thomas is a group facilitator and career advisor who has had the privilege of facilitating for over 20 years and providing Career Advisement/Job Readiness coaching for up to 5 years thus far. She started her career as a group facilitator at the age of 16 while serving on the Administration for Children Services Office of Youth Development Peer Leadership Council as a peer advocate for youth in foster care until she aged out of the system at the age of 21. Since she has had the privilege of facilitating in the non-profit sector in areas such as Education and Youth Development, Nutrition and Health, Employment and Career Readiness, and basic Financial Literacy. Ciara has a strong passion for seeing others succeed and displaying their true potential. Currently, she is in the process of taking her career to new heights as a freelance resume writer on Fiverr.com and as an entrepreneur starting her own job/career readiness training and services business through workshops in resume and cover letter writing, interview prep, and LinkedIn profile optimization. Ciara is a wife, mother, and Evangelist who loves the Lord and serving others. To contact her you can email her at resumingforward@gmail.com.

Helper Of Mankind
By Cassandra Keys

The meaning of my name, my whole life I tried to live up to it. At this particular time in my life's journey, one of my dear friends was having some issues in her marriage. It was closely leading to divorce. She and her husband decided to separate for a while. She and the children needed a place to stay. Of course, I extended a helping hand. She and the children would stay with me until she saved up enough money to get her an apartment.

She worked the night shift, and I worked the day shift. Again, I extended a helping hand and agreed to get the children ready for daycare and drop them off. I had it all planned out. I would get up an hour earlier than I usually did and get all of the children ready which were my three and her two toddlers. At the time my children were ten, nine, and six years old. They were in school all day.

I am a Superwoman. Let me explain. The daycare was in the opposite direction, so getting up an hour should be ok. Also part of the plan was she would get dinner ready, and I would give them baths and get everyone ready for bed. As my memory serves me, she only kept her part of the agreement only three times out of the three and half months she was there. I still had to stick with the plan because as a child, I was always taught your word is your bond, and all you have is your WORD. I hear those words coming out of my mom's mouth so vividly. With knowing that I had to do the best I could to make this work. As we would come home from school and work, she would not be there. She had to go in to work quite frequently early as she stated. This went on for about two weeks straight. Of course, I was extremely exhausted.

I had stopped going to church regularly and that caused my pastor to call me to see if I was okay. I talked with him about what was going on in my life. He advised me to pray about the situation and listen for the voice of God. I prayed and talked to God. I said, "Lord, I want to continue to help my friend, however, I am tired, and I am starting to neglect my own children because I am so tired. I prayed the same prayer for a week straight.

One day when I went to work, my supervisor said I could leave early. She told me to go get some rest and take a few hours to get some time to myself. As I was driving home, I don't know what made me drive past my friend's house. Her car was in the driveway. Of course, I was surprised. I called her and told her we needed to talk. We talked that morning, and I asked her why didn't she tell me she and her husband were back together. She said she was embarrassed because when we were teenagers we vowed never to take crap from a man. Since I was recently divorced, she thought I would say she wasn't strong. I explained to her wanting to work on her marriage shows that she is a strong woman, and I admired her. I also told her we didn't know anything about life when we made that statement about men. I divorced because of my husband's drug addiction (that's another book in the making).

To this date, I get a gift card for a massage from her and her husband. The note always says, "Thanks for your help, Queen." I have learned that when you help someone, make sure it will not affect you physically, mentally, or financially. I have a few Bible verses that I read when I am feeling a bit overwhelmed.

Joshua 1:9
Be Strong And Be Of Good Courage; Bet Not Afraid, Neither Be Thou Dismayed; For The Lord Thy God Is With Thee Whithersoever Thou Goest.

Proverbs118: 17
I Shall Not Die, But Live, And Declare The Work Of The Lord.

2Timothy 4:17
But The Lord Stood With Me And Gave Me Strength.
"My Peace Is Paramount. "

I leave you with this, Take the Cape Off, Sis..

About
Cassandra Keys

Cassandra Keys is a wife, mother, grandmother, friend, and motivator. She currently works in the medical field as a Surgical Processing Technician Supervisor. At a young age, she found her passion for the medical field while working as a Certified Nursing Assistant in a nursing home where her grandmother was a resident.

After a short time, she transferred to the hospital where she found enjoyment as a Sterile Processing Technician. She has now worked in the medical field for

29 years and is grateful to be a part of something that continuously helps others.

In addition to her passion for the medical field, she has also found joy in home décor and fashion. Her love for fashion has encouraged her to become a small business owner. She is the proud owner of Sista Queen Bead Boutique where she specializes in customized jewelry and fashionable clothes.

With the skillset and knowledge, she has gained over the years, she has been able to help so many people from all different walks of life. Helping others has been awesome and rewarding, but she realizes that in order to help others, she has to be at her best and make sure she is healthy and well to be the light in someone else's life.

Buried Deep
By Landai Barnes

Proverbs 3:5-8
Trust in the Lord with all your
Heart and lean not on your own understanding.
6) in all your ways submit to Him, and he will
Make Your paths straight. 7) Do not be wise in
your own eyes; Fear the Lord and shun evil. 8)
This will bring health to Your body and
nourishment to your bones.

As I sit and contemplate which part of my life to write about, I am reluctant to reveal it. It is not for fear of rejection or any kind of fear at all, for I have lived in fear and isolation most of my life. I am reluctant because there is so much that can be said about our strength and resilience as people. God doesn't make mistakes and it is because of God's love for me I was able to endure the hardships and pain that life brought me.

I started off lonely and alone and I used to think that I would be alone and lonely for the rest of my life. However, after a while, I chose to stay alone but not to stay lonely. I owe that all to the long, lasting, and loving words of God our Father which kept playing in my head. "You are not alone", "I will never leave you nor forsake you" and "I am with you wherever you.

See my biggest issue was the inability to communicate. I had a hard time trusting people and communicating my feelings and emotions maturely and effectively. I had the hardest time trusting myself, my thoughts, and my actions. I was my worst critic and hardest on myself and I had very negative conversations with myself daily that placed new pressures on me.

So, I will let you in on a colossal size secret, ARE YOU READY? Ok, here we go, Communication and forgiveness is key to a long-lasting and fulfilling relationship. Whether it is a friendship, companionship, and spouse/significant others. When a person harbors unforgiveness in their hearts they hurt themselves more than the other person. They don't get to free themselves from the anger, envy, animosity, stress, and bitterness that comes with unforgiveness. All of these things can have a great impact on your mental, emotional and physical health, as well as, the spiritual and financial areas in their lives.

However, what's just as big is a lack of communication. If you grew up in a house with little to no communication, then you may lack the ability to communicate effectively. So there was a childhood trauma that I experienced and as so many have experienced before me and will experience after me, there is just something that plays over and over in your head as it relates to that trauma. The more support you have the bigger the possibility of a full as possible recovery.

Soooo...as things started happening to me in my life growing up, I started harboring feelings of unforgiveness and anger towards my mother. "WHAT," you say, "How can you do that?" Well as most people know the person that is the closest to you will usually get the backlash for all things wrong in your life, even if they are only "passing along the baton." When I say "passing along the baton," I mean that there are things that have attached themselves to your family. Either through spirits or other people's words. These spirits and words have manifested themselves through your bloodline generations ago. Without the knowledge of God and the power of the Holy Spirit, we can't see it or understand the damage that it does within our families, nor see the generations of damage that has been done before and possibly after you. It's TIME TO BREAK these generational ties that connect us to these curses and spirits that have been attached to our family line. Which are also considered generational curses.

Please believe and understand that my mother was doing the best she could do under the circumstances and in the same manner that it was taught to her. So, why was I so angry? Why was I giving my mother so much hell? Well, I'm glad you asked. Well first, who else could I blame? The closest one to me was my mother at the time, and in my finite way of thinking, she was my protector, my provider, and who I wanted to spend time with. So my anger was warranted, it was a child's anger and my feelings and emotions were all over the place.

The one thing about communication is if you don't know how to communicate, then you can use the wrong emotions to communicate your thoughts and feelings. For example, a child who has not matured in certain areas of their lives can be angry because of something that happened at school or any other place outside of the house. So when they come home, if the person that they come home to doesn't know how to assist that child in communicating how they feel or even trying to find out why the child is angry, this can lead to situations and circumstances that can cause disconnection in the home. The authority figure may feel that the child is ignoring them or giving them attitude when asked to do something and will, in turn, respond in anger. This usually happens when a parent is preoccupied with other things in life and needs their child to do something. They have missed the opportunity to understand what the child is experiencing for lack of ability on how to communicate, or too busy and now there are two angry people in the house. One with power and one who is powerless. As adults, we tend to miss those signs and then a tug of war ensues and if we don't discuss what is going on it starts to breed isolation with the powerless. Then the powerless will begin to reach out to others in a need to be heard or to express themselves about what is happening.

So, hopefully you will see where I am going with this. As I was getting older, the need to be heard was becoming more profound. Due to the lack of communication in the home, I wanted to communicate but didn't know how and to whom. I felt stifled in my home, and it was affecting my mind, my heart, and my ability to feel like I belonged. I couldn't do one thing because my oldest brother did it, and he messed up. I couldn't do something else because my younger brother was watching me. So all I could do was go and read. Well now, who wants to always read, maybe sometimes, half the time or even most of the time but not all of the time. So when I reached 14, I wanted to leave. Now my trauma happened at age 7, so confusion started at that age coupled with misunderstanding and an inability to communicate my feelings and emotions. To top it all off, not having someone who is able to assist me in navigating my feelings and emotions. I craved communication, and I wanted to communicate.

I started latching onto people that were involved in another world I wasn't used to. As a result of my trauma, I started to become flirtatious, and sexual in order to communicate how I was feeling. My communication tactics led me to be spiritually entangled with people who didn't have my best interest at heart. Although there was a fear of how people would respond or judge me. I was a very sexual being, craving attention, and communication in the wrong way. It was bred out low self-esteem, low self-confidence, and low self-worth which came from feelings of abandonment, lack of communication, and harboring un-forgiveness and my trauma.

In my inability to communicate effectively with people on a verbal level, and my inability to be able to help people understand where I'm coming from, and with what was happening in my life I started to Harbor un-forgiveness. Un-forgiveness because I was misunderstood, misinformed and ill-educated. Un-forgiveness came on a different scale for me and because of my confusion and lack of the ability to communicate my feelings and emotions, my un-forgiveness started taking root in my heart. The un-forgiveness happened, first for the person who disrespected me, and then for the person who was supposed to protect me. Next, were the feelings of inadequacy, then layers of guilt, fear, insecurity, low self-confidence, low self-esteem, low self-worth and yes more un-forgiveness.

Here we have more un-forgiveness being harbored in my heart and it was again directed to the only person that was supposed to be there to protect me. My mother who should've been my hero, my mother who should've been my guide, my mother who should've been my lead, couldn't lead in the way that was needed for her little girl. A girl who went through some things at the hands of a monster, however, my mother was only able to lead in the best way she knew how. This way came from her past hurts and trauma. However, that is her story to tell.

All of those layers were weighing me down mentally, emotionally, physically and spiritually. All of these feelings were laying on top of the real issue and that issue was with the person who first hurt me. Being too young to know how to communicate to the people I needed to and the heaviness of un-forgiveness that controlled me. Then there came the resentments. I resented the person who harmed me, the person who was supposed to be there to protect me and anyone else who couldn't truly see what was going on or who couldn't help me. However, because I could not communicate effectively those feelings of anger and resentment started to meet with an isolation I couldn't control. This isolation was my ability to anchor myself against the world in an effort to protect myself because others were unable to protect me.

Communication is absolutely key to healing and is key to forgiveness. Without proper communication all things harmful will continue to fester inside and make headway for mental illness, emotional instability, physical sickness, spiritual blocks and financial inadequacies. All with which I've had to deal with. But God and I don't say that lightly, I say it with much conviction, "BUT GOD."

God has shown me who I am and has confirmed whose I am. So in my heart, in my mind, in my spirit and in my soul I now know whose I am and who I am. I am a child of the Most High God and I am fearfully and wonderfully made (Psalm 139:13-14) in his image and likeness. The Word says that I am the head and not the tail, I will be above and not beneath, that I will be the lender and not the borrower (Deuteronomy 28:12-13). The word says you shall reap what you sow (Galatians 6:7-8) and life and death lies in the power of the tongue (Proverbs 18:21). The Word says you are more than a conqueror in Christ (Romans 8:37), I can do all things through Christ Jesus which strengthens me (Philippians 4:13) and Create in me a clean heart O Lord and renew a steadfast spirit in me. Cast me not away from you your presence and do not take your spirit away from me (Psalm 51:10-13). The Word says, trust in the Lord with all your heart and lean not on your own understanding; in all your ways acknowledge him and he too shall direct your path (Proverbs 3:5-6). The word of God will never come back to him void (Isaiah 55:11) and the word of God is quick, and powerful, and sharper than any two edge sword (Hebrews 4:12). So my question to you is, "Whose Report will you believe? (Isaiah 53).

In closing, my prayer for you today is:

"Let the word of God take root in your heart, take hold of your mind and take the lead in your life, in Jesus name. Amen.

OUR DEEPEST FEAR
Marianne Williamson

"Our deepest fear is not that we are inadequate.
Our deepest fear is that we are powerful beyond
measure.
It is our Light, not our Darkness, that most frightens
us.
We ask ourselves, who am I to be brilliant, gorgeous,
talented, fabulous?
Actually, who are you not to be?
You are a child of God. Your playing small does not
serve the World.
There is nothing enlightening about shrinking
so that other people won't feel unsure around you.
We were born to make manifest the glory of God that
is within us.
It is not just in some of us; it is in everyone.
As we let our own light shine,
we consciously give other people permission to do
the same.
As we are liberated from our own fear,
our presence automatically liberates others."

About
Landai Barnes

If one was to describe Landai Barnes, they would say that she is a daughter, sister, granddaughter, niece, aunt, mother, cousin, friend, confidant, teacher, secretary, encourager, lifter up of spirits, steward, follower, leader, conqueror, an overcomer, an achiever, co-heir with Christ, a forgiver and most importantly a child of the most high God.

Landai Barnes was born and raised in the Bronx, NY and now resides in Newark, NJ. She is a mother of one young gentleman, Dominick Smith, whom she is proud to have had the pleasure of raising. She has overcome many obstacles and achieved many goals. The most recent one includes graduating from Nyack College with a Bachelor of Science in Social Work and is currently pursuing her Masters in Social Work (Clinical Studies). Since giving her life over to Christ she has been striving to better her walk with Christ and to encourage others to see their true potential and place in the Kingdom of God. She loves to talk about God and every conversation she has somehow begins and/or ends with God. She has been quoted as saying, "Who better to talk about than Jesus Christ who died for us, and God the Father who allowed it to happen. My job is not to talk about you, but to pray for you."

Landai was a member of Whosoever Will Ministries for 12 years and served as a secretary for the Women's Ministry, also known as the D.I.V.A.S ministry (Daughters of Integrity, Virtue, and Spirituality). She also served as a Sunday School teacher (ages 4 – 12) and was a member of the choir where she served as secretary.

Landai currently attends Bread of Life Kingdom Fellowship located in North Brunswick, NJ where she serves as a part of the Media & Arts Ministry. She also serves on the Levitical Worship Team and was currently consecrated as Minister of Worship. She believes that in order for the community to thrive we must build one person at a time.

With a greater desire to serve and build the kingdom of God, Landai can help others discover what their purpose is. She is passionate about spreading the good news through evangelism and serving others through the ministry gift of help (1 Cor. 12:28). Landai is very excited about all the things God has in store for her.

My Favorite Narc
By Sydney Nicholas

Something doesn't feel right...
I distinctly remember telling a friend of mine that there was something wrong with my husband. At the time, I thought it was due to his illness. He had not been taking care of himself. My friend, who was in the medical field, gave me some things to check for to see if there was any neurological damage being caused by his neglect.

He was just mean for mean's sake. Or rather he was meaner than usual. I dismissed it a little as this was our cycle. He would be nasty and then sweet and attentive. Then back to nasty. There would be periods of extra nasty to the point that I would want to leave, but I never did because you just don't leave a marriage. You work things out. That's what my family demonstrated. That's what I stuck with. He wasn't physically abusive. He was unfaithful but we were working that out. So, why so mean and spiteful?

When I sat back to think about it, I realized it was something that had been going on for a while and I did not recognize it. Something just wasn't right. I kept having those moments where I would notice little things that didn't add up. Gaps in his stories. Quips that he would dismiss as jokes but did not sit that way. Lies for lying sake. Being wholly insensitive and feigning ignorance of the offense. Blaming me for taking his cruel remark the wrong way. I was too sensitive.

When I broached the subject with him about his behavior, I was told that I was crazy. It was all in my mind. I'm getting upset over nothing. I'm seeing things that were not there. This one was my favorite because it was the excuse he used to cover the affair that ultimately sent me packing. Even his friends would talk to me sideways, and it was then that I realized that he had been talking crazy about me to other people. This started when I started to see who and what he really was.

He is an undiagnosed covert narcissist. A covert narcissist is extremely sensitive to criticism of any kind because they feel that they are perfect and better than everyone. A covert narcissist is passive-aggressive. They do not have outbursts like other people. They hold grudges and wait for the opportunity to get revenge. Revenge will manifest by either giving the silent treatment, mocking the offender in mixed company or causing drama with a common friend or associate, with the offender being the bad guy. Since doing anything selfless is not for their benefit, they will procrastinate or flat out not perform favors of any kind unless there is some kind of benefit.

Covert narcissists come across as self-deprecating and almost humble. The goal here is so that someone can console them and tell them how great they are. After all, no one wants to be around someone downing themselves. They are withdrawn almost to shyness because they don't want someone getting close enough to see their failures. The only reason they would let someone get close to them, as in my case to marriage, is because there is a benefit to the other person being there. In my case, I took care of everything. I have a heart for community in my home and service, and I won't just sit around and not contribute to the house. Sadly, I worked overtime because I was constantly being accused of doing nothing because I didn't follow his schedule of activities.

Like all narcissists, they have delusions about their own grandeur. They are constantly thinking and talking about their abilities being superior to other people. You may even catch them in an "I'll show you" moment. They can be very envious of other people they feel can challenge their superiority. Because they have made themselves larger than they are, they tend to suffer from feelings of inadequacy. They cannot meet their own high expectations.

They don't have really deep relationships because they lack empathy. In fact, whatever compassion or empathy they do show is a mirror of what they have seen from someone else and it is an act. They never want to be seen as unlikeable. Their helpfulness and generosity stem from their desire to be admired. However, this is not real, and more than likely, that friend that is the covert narcissist is not a real personality at all. They are just mirroring you so that you feel you have more in common than you actually do.

I Almost Gave Up...

I had gotten to the point of giving up. I had resigned myself to being this doormat. I was convinced that I was lucky to have anyone. I had gained so much weight that I was almost 300 lbs. I felt unwanted. He made sure I knew that everything I did was wrong to the point that I had to check with him before doing anything. In true narcissist form, he kept me off balance. I was so undone, I was becoming forgetful, and he used it like a champ. Moving things around on me, saying that he told me things he never did.

He would buy the most unattractive clothes and say I looked great in them. I would look at the same garment and wonder if there was something wrong with his eyes. But, then I would blame myself for being ungrateful. Some husbands don't buy their wives anything. So, it's not exactly my style but, it's the thought that counts, right? Totally negating the fact that it was the least he could do since I literally paid for everything. He didn't think that he should do anything so whatever I asked he would procrastinate doing it to the point that I would end up doing it myself. He would then blame me for doing everything and not asking him to do anything.

We had a brief separation because of a short-lived affair but he came back, hat in hand, promising me the world with apologies that I was needing to hear, and he knew that. He was away long enough to make me docile and pliable for his return but not long enough for me to remember who I was and figure out who I was becoming. But he was gone long enough for me to see God standing to the side waiting for me to turn my head.

A Turning Point...

I describe covert narcissists as patient people. Most of the research I've done on the subject, the victims were in a relationship with them for many years. Much like in my case. So, how did I discover this was the issue? I wish I could say that I wised up on my own. The only thing I can say is that it was God, and God alone. I was online reading an email, and I clicked out into an article. I don't remember what it was about but at the bottom of the article where the related articles were was a headline that caught my attention.

I still don't remember the headline. It was something innocuous but intriguing enough to get my attention. So, I read the article. You know that feeling you get when something happens, and the air changes around you? That feeling that makes your stomach drop and time stop for a split second when you realize that something has not been right for a while. You have finally gotten a lead on what has been happening. That's the feeling I had after I read that article.

It was about narcissism. This was my a-ha moment. I sat back in my chair, and I took a deep breath. I could have sworn the writer of the article had been living in my house and was writing about my life and my marriage. What didn't connect though, was the fact that the writer was calling the experience abuse.

Speaking for myself, when I think of the word abuse, my mind immediately goes to physical or sexual abuse.

It didn't dawn on me that there were other categories. What was happening to me couldn't have been abuse, could it? Because the article was so close to home, I had to figure out what narcissism was and what the different types meant. The more I dug, the more I began to kick myself. It's a hard pill to swallow, knowing that the person you fell in love with was not real. It's tough to know that you built a life with someone that doesn't really exist. You need to come to terms with the fact that you will never get an apology or any type of closure, for that matter. Even more difficult is the fact that there was nothing that could have helped you avoid this because you are a loving and open-hearted person. As I dug deeper, I stopped blaming myself for whatever insecurity that I had that kept him in my life to wreak such havoc, and I started to rethink my position that perhaps it was abuse.

After reading that article, I got curious. There is no open spotlight on mental and emotional abuse. In fact, what I know of it, I got from psychological thriller movies. But, I was always able to see the crazy right away and yell at the actors to run. They never heard me. Just like no one ever heard me because I was "groomed" not to run and to welcome the killer into my home.

It took some time and another separation due to another affair before I would be almost convinced of the label of covert narcissist. It took some time to wrap my head around the fact that I was abused. In my experience, these types of things were covered by things like, "that's just how they are." They were presented in a manner that we should just deal with it and move on. It was never described as abusive behavior that should not be tolerated.

The second separation was much longer, and I had time to draw closer to God and discover my purpose. I was able to take a step back and figure out who I was and what I needed to do. I healed from most of the scars that I carried. My children were flourishing. When, he came back for round three, I was ready.

I just couldn't bring myself to just label him a covert narcissist. I felt like I had not done all I could to reach him. In my experience, the word narcissist was just a name we gave self-centered people. The people who did nothing but talk about themselves and what they were doing. They had no inkling that anyone else was there, just that there were people listening. Those are the overt ones. The ones we can spot from a mile away. Never did I think there was a lesser brother with all the qualities and none of the blatant warning signs until you are hooked. Amazingly enough, the overt narcissist is the one you would prefer should you encounter one.

The covert narcissist presents as someone who is almost humble. I struggled on several fronts dealing with him after I realized what was happening. We had known each other since we were kids and he was the love of my life. I remembered how he checked off all my boxes and appeared to be my perfect counterpart. I also remembered how he acted during our first separation, and I realized that it was a discard. He treated me like I was just someone he used to know. Not someone with whom he spent over a decade.

Naturally, some decisions had to be made. I spent the last go-round coming to terms with the last vestiges of hope that I was not dealing with what I was dealing with. I spent that time fighting my Goliath, my husband. Until this point, I don't think I really stood up to him. I spent the last separation with God. Learning and studying the Word. Filling my mind and spirit with the things of God. If there was any doubt about the transforming power of the Word of God, I am a witness.

I no longer felt like I was breaking those unspoken rules of breaking up my home. I placed a premium on keeping my family together. After spending time in the Word I knew that surely God did not mean for me to stay in this place. I realized that God actually answered a prayer I forgot I prayed. I simply asked Him to show me who were the people around me. When I think back, He showed me who everyone was in my circle. My husband was no different, and it was just before I saw the article that changed everything.

About a year before the last separation God brought a verse to my attention: 1 Corinthians 7:15. It says, *But if the unbelieving depart, let him depart. A brother or a sister is not under bondage in such cases: but God hath called us to peace.* (KJV) It was as if Jesus himself came into my house and said, "Peace. Be still." This verse hit me because 1.) God was telling me that my husband was leaving, and I was relieved, and 2.)

God was telling me that even the faith my husband professed to have been developing was not there. It was jarring. Not even the so-called belief in God he was holding was real.

It's funny though. God is so merciful to all his children. Even though, my husband was considered an unbeliever, He gave my husband the opportunity to repent. We cannot forget that even unbelievers are God's creation. My husband's reply was more of the same to the point of doubling down in some areas and the orchestration of biblical grounds for our parting. I don't need to tell you I am free of him, do I?

Two Truths and a Lie (Well, several lies)...

Hebrews 4: 12 says *For the word of God is quick, and powerful, and sharper than any two-edged sword, piercing even to the dividing asunder of soul and spirit, and of the joints and marrow, and is a discerner of the thoughts and intents of the heart.* (KJV)

I was afforded the opportunity to spend a year unattached to anyone or anything except my children, my job, and God. I did have a few sessions of therapy over the years but this year, I did not need it. My time spent with God was an extraordinary experience. I found peace. I found joy. I found me. I held on to two things which I am calling my two truths.

Truth #1: Psalm 139:14 (KJV) says *I will praise thee; for I am fearfully and wonderfully made: marvellous are thy works; and that my soul knoweth right well.* I don't know about you but this verse blessed my soul. Once I understood my place in God's heart, this verse took on new meaning. I had been living for so long under this thought of being less, that I did not value myself. I allowed my worth and my being to be subject to another person's mercurial approval. I was convinced that I was nothing and would be nothing and would have nothing. After meditating on this verse and coming to the understanding that God designed each and every one of us the way we are on purpose with a purpose in mind.

Every curve I have, He thought of and made provision for. I am beautiful no matter what anyone says. The way my mind works is just the way God needed it to function. My accomplishments were the stuff to make Jesus stand up for me. Not an accusation to make other people feel bad. I was shown how to run my house, manage my money, who the people around me were.

When this was understood, all of what I was trying to do fell into place. Everything came together as it should. In addition to being fearfully and wonderfully made, add Matthew 6:33 to this first truth because it was the first thing that I did. *But seek ye first the kingdom of God, and his righteousness; and all these things shall be added unto you.* (KJV) When I tell you all things work together for the good of them that love the Lord and are called according to His purpose, it is the absolute truth.

Your enemies have no idea that they work for God on a regular basis. One thing the narcissist does is isolate you. They leave no one for you to turn to. No one to talk to. You almost become just as fake as they are in that respect. However, in the very position of having no one you can talk to, you have God. God loves when He has your undivided attention. He was the first person I spoke to because another fun thing you experience is shame for having been duped. You're too embarrassed to tell anyone all that you have been putting up with. It's even more so with a covert narcissist because you could literally be with them for years before you see any of the traits manifest.

Remember, there is no condemnation in the kingdom of God so tell Him everything!

Truth #2: Romans 12:19 (KJV) says *Dearly beloved, avenge not yourselves, but rather give place unto wrath: for it is written, Vengeance is mine; I will repay, saith the Lord.*

One of the things that totally threw me was the level of anger I experienced. It was closer to rage. Rage at one simple fact: he knows exactly what he was doing and is not fazed by it in the least. In fact, he thrived off my misery. When I realized that little tidbit, I started trying to plan a revenge scenario for the ages. So that he truly felt all the years he stole, all the love he tossed into the trash and the good times never had. One day as I was reveling in my revenge fantasy God simply said, "It won't matter." I snapped right out of my daydream and yelled at God like Jonah. "Whatchu mean God?" He simply turned my attention to Romans 12:19.

God does not want his children to suffer or to be mishandled in any way. While the bible does not say the word abuse, it does speak to all the specific ways we can be abused so that there is no ambiguity to what He means. What is clear in all those verses is that 1.) God does not and will never support you being abused. So, if you are being abused ask God to stand up in you and leave. Ask God to go before you to make a way that is protected for your departure. 2.) When you spot people that misuse others, don't mix with them. Psalm 1 says not only don't mix with them but you are blessed for following that simple guide. 3.) Never tolerate people that misuse you. The bible says to pray for the people that despitefully use you not spend as much time possible with them.

And now the lie...

Everything that your abuser said or did to make you feel small, unwanted, unvalued, and less than the child of the Most High that you are. You are a treasure to the Lord. You are royalty. You have a purpose on this earth. You were put here for such a time as this!

Meditation: 1 Peter 2:9 KJV
But ye are a chosen generation, a royal priesthood, an holy nation, a peculiar people; that ye should shew forth the praises of him who hath called you out of darkness into his marvellous light;

About
Sydney Nicholas

Sydney Nicholas is a blogger, author, podcaster, chocolatier, and lover of God's people. She was born in Manhattan, NY, and raised in the Bronx. Growing up during a time when rap music was blossoming and jazz, R&B, and the arts were staples in the city community, she naturally became a concert pianist and cellist.

Sydney relocated to central Florida to begin her adventure of raising her family where she also discovered her love of food and became a pastry chef and chocolatier. She rekindled her love of writing and discovered her newfound love of God.

Sydney has become the leader of the Crosstown Christian Assembly's Diamonds and Pearls Women's Ministry. She is the founder and main writer for LiveSelah.com and host and creator of the podcast, Conversations of the Soul. She has also written a devotional, While In the Valley: Encouragement While You Go Through, and is expected to release Of Faith and Trees in 2022. These titles are written under S. Marie Nicholas.

When she is not writing, podcasting, or creating delicious artisan chocolate, she is teaching and empowering women to embrace the woman God intended them to be without apology.

The New Mandate is Love
By Sabrina J. Lewis

She led with a smile instilling principles of honor and love first in her home. It was known that if a phone call, pop-up meeting, or letter was to be scheduled or composed She was the one to do it. Love in action is her; at work, school, in community, or ministry. She communicates clearly with persistence, courage, and love. One can learn much just by observation, if ever around her there is a life lesson to be learned. She is you and She is in me. She's the ultimate Leadher in wisdom & forever our Sunshine.

This world has been consistent in telling others what to do. How dare one force another to do anything that may go against his or her belief, moral, or desire. If there is to be a mandate, it should be with laws that naturally govern this earth. A mandate should first begin within. When looking at ourselves in a mirror we ought to have gratitude for all that we are. We've been taught to seek validation from outside worlds in diverse forms oftentimes ending up broken, confused, and abused. I say no more, and now decree a new mandate beginning effective immediately, calling on LOVE!

The greatest gift and highest commandment is love. Many were taught that serving, literally to death is love. This world has drastically misunderstood that context, and turned love into active variations of slavery. When giving or providing a service out of pure joy, and not for a title or a status, this is love. When it feels right according to instinct meaning your heart and mind connects, then keep going! You're working on the right path towards destiny. Yet if there's any feeling of discomfort, stop immediately and run away. End it, whatever it may be. You hold the power.

Before we get started grab your highlighters, a pen, and some water. Be sure to journal or document anything that may speak to you along this journey.

This chapter is dedicated to the Sunshine in My Soul, Momma Judy Lewis, My Family (so thankful we have each other) as well every Lead*her* around the world, and Anyone currently holding this book in hand.

The Story begins

It all started in Brooklyn 2005 in a discussion with one of my best friends from high school. The phone conversation was long and brief at the same time in regards to relocating to build my dream of a wellness empire. It included my dream home, businesses, and eventually marrying "the" dream man. In less than 20 minutes I searched for a job, called ahead to introduce myself, and to see if it was still available. I was told to submit my résumé after a brief conversation and I did. An interview was set up that next week or so, if only I could find my journal from 2005; however, time and space are limited at this moment so I may retract in a later book or interview with more details on this part of the story so stay connected.

Family and friends celebrated my relocating to the ATL! I flew out, settled in, and prepared for my interview. I was hired, and begin working immediately! It was a bittersweet experience in East Cobb Marietta back in 2005. I worked in a white-owned and operated beauty salon. There were no black clients. This was more than OK considering my training was done in the city of New York with a focus only on Caucasian hair. At the time I'd mastered the basics of cultural diversity, customer service, haircutting, coloring, and other cosmetology services. I only had to be an apprentice to achieve the required hours for the state board of Georgia. It was imperative though that I master various round brush blow-dry styling techniques. So over time y'all, Sis did that! Other than the burn of the blow, and some minor prejudices, this job was perfect for me.

Super excited I began working my buns off with big goals to build a hair salon, spa, and merge it with wellness and naturopathic services. I was literally singing the song, "closer to my dreams," (by Goapele). Over time, Momma was concerned that I was alone, and should have a bodyguard. Although a bit much to me, Ma informed me of a dear friend of hers who had family that I should connect with and a long short story I did.

We end up dating, he moves in with me, we move back to Brooklyn, I get a new job, and move back with mom and dad. We're still dating, we get pregnant, and then I pray! I did not believe either of us was ready to be married. I knew we weren't the best match for each other. The next few weeks were challenging, I had a miscarriage. Although a sad experience, this was the confirmation I needed to progress forward. Over time we mutually ended the relationship.

I found out the miscarriage was due to hyperthyroidism. I was diagnosed with 2 enlarged goiters on both left and right thyroid glands at the time. I did not agree with the illness. I also did not agree with Doctors telling me I'd be on medication for the rest of my life. So I became a health researcher to manifest my own goals. I began looking for native remedies not only this time for family and friends as I have for decades, but now for myself. Upon testing out various remedies I became my own healer.

Although I began nursing myself back to health in Brooklyn, I knew the business still had to be established in Georgia. I needed to get back by any means necessary. I was thoroughly disappointed for allowing myself to be distracted, as well for listening to others who had not the vision or understanding of my divine assignment.

I worked in Brooklyn for a while then headed back to Georgia with childhood friends. This time I'm on the sofa working a home decor 3rd management position in the mall because it was the quickest thing I could find at the time. Sis had to be independent so I did that for a while then, I came back to New York. Worked it out again for a while, and then went back to Georgia; same friends, different location. This time I had been to Clayton County and now Emory Buckhead and would have my own.

I needed a car so researched, and called the nearest dealership. After getting pre-approved with a guarantor, a representative picked me up to purchase my new 2008 KIA Rio, This was in 2007. Super excited I began looking the same day for a home. I found a really nice community with a pool, fitness, and business centers. Finally, I ended up moving into my beautiful one-bedroom garden home soon after. This space was perfect for me. I embraced the community which had a Whole Foods market, Barnes & Noble, post office, library, and a really cool thrift shop among other necessities I frequently used. My unit was cozy, on ground level with a terrace. I had a washer and dryer too y'all this was lovely to me. My very 1st home. Everyone who knows me knows how I feel about doing laundry outside of my home.

So now I was "Ms. Independent" (by Neo) for real! had a car, my own home, a job at the mall, then picked up another night job doing data entry during tax season at Bank of America. I hustled doing hair, and wellness evenings and weekends. I enjoyed each moment of aloneness. As time passed I hit a rough patch and went to stay with a family friend in Stone Mountain. I received a call that Grandma was not well, and Mom was in the hospital so I go home and stay longer than a little while. Eventually, I completely gave up my apartment, both jobs, and returned home to NYC

I cared for Grandma and Ma, met a handsome smart man, fell in love, and gave birth to our Prince Love in August 2009, Grandma passed away in July 2009. Life began changing super-fast. I had to begin adulting in ways I wasn't ready for. Fast forward, the next year, 2010 Prince Love's Dad also transitioned August 7th to a homicide. I was in denial for a while although I knew the reality of what had transpired. I reminisced and was thankful for the time I had in Georgia, yet knew I was needed at home for a while.

I stayed with Mom and Dad to be nurtured through stages of deep disappointment and sorrow. Sunshine was devastated that I could experience love, go through trials, and then bury him all so fast. Her heart was truly broken for me. Thankful for family and Rapha Evangelistic Worship Center at the time, I grew in wellness. I began teaching group fitness and hosting health and wellness workshops catered to community developments. We've transitioned through the years to Rapha Art Life Center now bringing healing modalities and spreading love everywhere we go. It really is home to interfaith personalities all over this world. Visit us at Rapha-tv.org. There has been so much spiritual growth and life skills gained from being in this space. In Honor of My Momma we have just launched The Judy Sunshine Youth Center where Kids Are People Too! We've met many beautiful souls these past 20+ years who have contributed beautifully to my soul wellness and Prince Loves as well.

I left NY again around 2015 for Atlanta, then again in 2017. I was never comfortable staying too long without my family so I came home for the new year 2017. The Caretaking process started in 2008 with Grandma, yet continued to January 2022 when our Sunshine Transitioned on the 13th. Now There's Dad, my siblings, and my family. Yet Ma gave me the approval and prayer of release prior to her passing this earthly realm to go live my dreams and that is exactly what I'm doing now with her Angelic host by my side.

I feel a new burning desire for life on the inside. A new mandate of love is beginning. Mom and I experienced many highs and lows with her illness, yet She kept on moving and smiling through it all. There is so much I'd like to share yet I must bring this to a close. I am thankful for friendships and community. Big Shout out to My Sis, Andrenee Boothe, for believing that my words would be a gift to this project. A Big thank you to my family and dear Sister friends who remained close and consistently reached out during this time. Shaquan Hoke thank you for obeying your instincts in putting this Anthology together. I have complete gratitude for the ability to write my way out of grief. I hope that as you read you will learn how to experience a deeper love of self with divine joy and self-care for your new beginnings.

I want you to know that your dreams may have been deferred, yet there will be a perfect time to work on your gifts. Momma always said that life begins at 40 (telling my age now). She let me know that she was proud of all that I will do in the near future based on her experiences with me while she was able to travel. We had a ball and I have no regrets. Everything that we need we already have within, so do not worry. This is the right divine time to go and do the dream. Sometimes we do not understand why things are happening the way they do when they happen. I've learned to surrender to the process. Now I have multimillionaire coaches and mentors waiting to build community with me when I am ready to relocate to Atlanta. The vision has only gotten bigger and better. I will complete my current work in Brooklyn, while planning effectively to WIN when I do officially relocate to Georgia (in my very near future).

Caring for the Lead*her* within

Everyone is talking about self-care and wellness saying; learn how to eat properly, make sure you move your body, drink your water, remove anything stressing you out, and get 8-9 hours' sleep. While valid, many of you know that you can have all the self-care in the world yet if daily living activities are not taken care of you will worry yourself into a heart attack. If you are not leading with love and money you will be unhappy. When able to manage finances effectively, knowing bills are paid there is no headache or migraine. Having financial education and literacy will encourage successful appropriations of self-love and care. Manage your financial wellness.

When a loved one falls ill you want to make sure that loved one has food, clean clothes, medication, holistic remedies, a comfortable atmosphere, and proper support in the forms of aid or assistance. Funds tend to go towards immediate needs. What if you lose income or your job along the journey of caretaking and begin living off of reserves that begin to run out? How do you maintain self-care? Well, listen! I've been there! guilty of running to take care of everything but my responsibilities. Yes, y'all I'm guilty of attending functions I could not afford, taking Uber or Lyft and not MTA, guilty yes of ordering food instead of cooking the groceries recently purchased! Super guilty of ordering on Amazon when I needed to do laundry. Overall quilt of negligence will haunt you.

We wear these big-ass heavy capes that feel like weights often smothering our very existence. On top of working diligently to maintain daily living necessities and some activities, we also work to maintain love, and relationships which can be extremely exhausting yet desired. They say there's compromise in love. While for some this may be true. I believe if we have the divine right partner (under grace and in perfect ways), then there will be more support than disappointment in this particular arena. Yet this is supposed to be a chapter if I continue on this roundabout it will be an entire book!

So, how do we Love Lyfe Well? Thorough disappointments, griefs, and random losses. It comes with first understanding who we are, and what we want. When we understand in detail all about ourselves within; who we are right now, who we were, what we want, adhering to the laws of the universe, then we are able to appropriately sift towards those desires becoming a reality. When it's time to make the appropriate shift we can do so because we know who we are. In case you've forgotten let me remind you! We are our ancestors' wildest dreams. While we don't have anything to prove to each other, we want to be successful according to our heart's true desire. So we write the vision so that we can understand it, and be able to explain it in less than 1 minute. We keep it simple and in the words of my Uncle Douglas, "We do it, then it will become a big hit." No limits!

Caring for the leader within forces us to quiet down in moments of solitude: curtains closed, writing pen in hand, with notebooks water, blanket throws, shawls, and whatever else makes us comfortable. My current situation is the above, along with water and 432 Hz frequency vibrations playing in the background to keep me uplifted and inspired along this writing journey. Caring for self-causes us to consider actions and love towards ourselves. It makes us introspect and think about how we've been treating ourselves. It's dimensional. We really have to sit down to de-compartmentalize our entire lives to assess what's really is going on. There's a difference between feelings and emotions. I've learned through these last six months of caring for my mom and living past her transition that we really do have the power to change our situation according to our thoughts and our words. We can practice self-care all we want, we can take a vacation, we can go shopping, we can eat healthier, we can exercise, have sex and drink our wine. We can do all the things that we're supposed to; however, if we're doing these things yet speaking against what we are seeking to accomplish it will all be in vain.

I will share some daily habits and rituals that comfort my soul wellness.

1. **Drink water.** I think about any possible dreams had the night before, I think about any thoughts

and ideas that are coming through my head and write them down. I am silent with closed eyes. I deep breathe coherently (sitting up back straight- stomach should protrude out, feet planted on the floor), counting backward from 6 to 1, Inhale 6-5-4-3-2-1 exhale, inhale 1-2-3-4-5-6-7-8- 9-10 exhale, Inhale 1-2-3-4-5-6-7-8-9-10, and hold, exhale 1-2-3-4-5-6-7-8-9-10, and then sit in silence. If there are any distractions I'll deeply inhale and then sing a long note, "La La La La La La La La La La La La La La La Laaaaaaaaaaaaaaaaaaaaaaaaaaaaa" in the form of an, exhale until focused on breaths and meditation. I repeat as necessary and then silence again. In meditation lies the truth, there's no hiding. We see ourselves clearly; what we're doing, and what we are not doing. It is the ultimate humbling experience. When we can be honest in these moments change begins.

2. **Meditations, affirmations, and prayers go together.** I started a midnight map conference line at 712.770.5289 # 979-126 as well via zoom, Meeting ID: 7931409022, Passcode: umv26w many decades ago. Although it wasn't midnight when it first started around 5 AM. We may be on a different prayer time or watch. There will always be a divine prayer time that works best or is called upon for your specific journey no matter where you are or what you doing. You must write. When you see on paper what you

see in your mind, the possibilities are inspiring, it makes you want to create. Whether positive or negative we must acknowledge what we see in order to progress in this life. YouTube can help in learning how to begin meditations and the same with affirmations. I'll share some of my favorites below! I love listening to Mekhi_El via Instagram.com/raphaartlifecenter, and Rev Ike, Dr. Cindy Trimm, Florence Scovel, and Eckhart Tolle to name a few on Youtube.

I open up my windows and allow fresh air into my space, I light my Santo and sage, while the windows are open. I give thanks in the form of dance, turn on some inspirational music that I could stretch to, and dance to. I flow to the healing rhythms obeying my bodily instincts, stretching, and breathing into each body system. I do this for at least 15 to 30 minutes daily. Most times I get so enthused once started it could last up to two hours! I'm definitely thankful when I wake up super early on those days lol #DanceForLife #CelebrateLife #BeHappy

3. **Plan.** Every Sunday I do a weekly review of what I know needs to be done for that week. Then daily I review the night before bed breaking it down to make sure that I focus on what's important now #TheWINformula. We do not want to be busy, we want results! My lists used to be so ridiculously long I'd be happy to check

off one or two items from the list. Now I put no more than three items on my list to do every day. I have four solid hours focused on work, another 3-four on homeschool, another four on business, the other four focused on home and family, and 1-2 hours focused on community. It really is true that when you fail to plan, well there's no winning in that so let's just win with real actionable plans to get results.

4. **Get help.** I've hired housekeepers, and assistants. My family has hired a chef and even drivers to support our lifestyles along mini journeys. At this time, I have mentors and coaches literally for just about every dimension of my life. I have therapists and counselors to help with grief and everyday concerns to a financial advisor, personal trainers as well business coaches, spiritual teachers, and healers.

5. **I take herbal bubble baths at least 3-4 times per week** with my favorite essential oils, hydrating my skin internally and externally with my favorite Shea butter oil mix (homemade), and my TLC wellness products. Water is life internally as well externally.

6. **I have seniors who are filled with wisdom that I get lots of life lessons from to help me make the best decisions for my life.** The point

here is we don't have all the answers. While we are striving for excellence, we need help along the way. So be not be afraid to reach out for help. They say, focus on your strengths while building your weaknesses. I say, obey your instincts and do what you know you need to do for yourself!

Repeat The Following Statements Out Loud Daily

1. I open up my hear and I open up my mind to receive all the good that I deserve and desire.
2. Everything always works out for me and all is well
3. I have everything I need and there is no lack in the kingdom.
4. My supply comes from God and now appears like mushrooms overnight, there are no hard times in the kingdom
5. I am now immune to all hurt, and resentment my poise is built upon a rock of love within.
6. I give and it is given back to me, pressed down, shaken together shall ben pour into my bosom, I give thanks for my immediate supply.
7. The Lord is my light in salvation whom shall I fear.
8. I control my conditions through word and thought, I speak only that which I desire to see and I think positive thoughts.

9. God appreciates me therefore man appreciate me nothing can interfere with my godly divine success.
10. I only desire that which infinite intelligence desires for me and I claim that which is mine by Divine right and under grace in perfect ways.
11. God's invincible power sweeps all over me, I ride the waves into my Promise land.
12. I love life, and life loves me. Life takes pleasure in my prosperity.

My new favorite poem given me from Momma Sunshine is "Footprints" With the actual visual.

I enjoyed spending time with you! Unlimited Blessings & love on your journey until we meet again. Before leaving, I'd like to gift you a free e-book, "A cup at a time" Visit sabrinajlewis.com and join the Love Lyfe Well community! Stay tuned to my next book on wellness and more to come.

#TheNewMandateIsLove
#Lovelyfewell & #Live
#TakeTheCapeOffSis

~SJL~

About
Sabrina J. Lewis

Sabrina J Lewis is a Visionary Leader, Ambassador, and Liaison of nations. She combines wellness, and worlds of beauty, through theory, practice and advocacy; additionally, her humanitarian work has been recognized by clergy, politicians, and community leaders.

As former Community Liaison & Public Health Worker in Pediatrics Sickle Cell at NYC Health +

Hospitals Systems, Sabrina hosted blood drives and educational wellness workshops that helped save over 600+ lives. She currently works with Sickle Cell Thalassemia Patient Network (SCTPN) under Sickle Cell Disease Association of America (SCDAA), via Kings County Hospital Adult Clinic developing partnerships, and connecting community members to medical homes and care.

Sabrina founded the Sickle Cell and Trait Support Group at Kings County Hospital in Brooklyn, NY to provide education and further assistance to families and individuals with supportive social services. Now called, "Sickle Cell and Trait Meets" the group has expanded into NYS Health + Hospitals Systems, with translation services available for attendees in need. Members also coordinate care nationwide online. The group meets every 2nd & 4th Tuesday at Noon with ongoing group engagement in WhatsApp. Email Sabrina.sctpn@gmail.com to get connected.

Sabrina served as Health Committee Chair for The Brooklyn Branch NAACP (National Association for the Advancement of Colored People), advocating health equities in public policy, access to healthy foods, affordable and quality care. Sabrina serves as a Trustee at Rapha Evangelistic Worship Center and Ambassador/ Community Organizer at Rapha Art Life Center in Brooklyn NY. She is also a local Community Board 9 Member of the Health & Social Service Committee in Brooklyn.

Sabrina enjoys the convenience of being a home school Mom to an Amazing Indigo Prince, and a Caretaker to loved ones. She is certified and licensed in the fields of wealth, wellness and beauty. Her Love Lyfe Well initiatives to bring information, access, education, products, and services supports families and communities building assets in NYC, Atlanta and is expanding. Her evenings and weekends are dedicated to community giving, educating on whole wellness, and providing beauty services. Email lovelyfewell@gmail.com to inquire.

When Sabrina is not working She enjoys reading in the book club and connecting with Ladies in the "I Am A Woman" Facebook community group She Founded. Her therapies are roller skating and traveling. She loves nature walks through the botanical gardens and spends quality time with her family in Brooklyn, NY and throughout the world.

Becoming
By Tamekia Victory

I wasn't always so enthusiastic about life. I enjoy watching others blossom developing their craft or notch. In fact, I was a dependable cheerleader when it came to encouraging others to follow their dreams while silencing my own dreams and goals due to my limiting beliefs. There was a constant inner voice that said, "You will never be enough." It was hard for me to accept good things happening for me without thinking there must be a gloomy situation just around the corner of my life. I was the "This is too good to be true kind of girl." Too scared to take a risk so I became complacent, never doing too much. I managed to remain just below the radar of attracting too much attention. Well, let me tell you how that all began to change. I was determined to fight for my life physically, mentally, spiritually, and emotionally. By right I was supposed to be counted OUT. I didn't fit the bill to be a success or to inspire anyone.

I have been a heavy weight much of my life. I thought this was how life would be for me. Not to mention I never thought I'd live passed my 20's. The things that we think about as kids are influenced by our environment and upbringing. I have always done what I was told to do with very little pushback. I was a people pleaser. I enjoyed being noticed for doing what was good, being kind and humble. These are all great characteristics that are even better when you know who you are, the problem is I didn't know who I was. I depended heavily on others telling me who I was and what I should do. I was overly dependent on others and living life through other people's eyes. This is not a sob story but one of victory to help you lose yourself of the self-sabotaging stories you may be telling yourself.

In 2016, I made one of the biggest decisions I've had to make in life. I left my secure job as a preschool head teacher to pursue my education full time in an effort to complete my bachelor's degree in education. This decision did not come easy. I was not happy and my performance at work was being affected. I second-guessed myself and the decisions I was making in the classroom daily. No one seemed to notice because I learned how to put up a front, faking it until I made it. Simultaneously I was feeling stuck in a rout in other areas of my life. Something was not right, but I couldn't quite put my finger on it. I mean I had a beautiful family, a well-paying teaching position, and things were going great at church. Well, the truth be told I was very unhappy making everyone else happy but myself. So, I was finally going to take a risk and do something I felt I needed to do "move on". I told my then director that it was "Now or Never".

I was moving on from what others thought I should be. What confirmed my decision was the prophetic release of a burden in my life during a church service. The woman servant of God spoke these words to me "God said the burden is lifted." I received those words and began to praise God and I literally had the feeling of a weight being taken off my body. From that moment to the present, I have encountered Destiny helpers and I will speak more about that soon. I also realized how God is the orchestrator of my life and life is so much better with him than without him.

I pondered the burden that this woman of God could have been talking about, I don't think I was ready to have an honest conversation with myself. I was completely broken. I had every label tagged to my life that I could think of. I specifically remember people loved me for the front that I had put up but within I was truly hurting. "You are not enough ringing in my ears, the more it rang the more I did to prove this voice wrong. Have you ever experienced just going through the motions of life but not being aware of life? "Well, if I do this, this, this, and this I am sure I will be accepted." I thought. I felt better and was moving in the right direction. I was taking time to complete my education. I was home a few days a week to be with my then one-year-old son and six-year-old daughter. That year we were financially stable. I even started a gym membership and hubby purchased us a pre-owned vehicle that was just like new with only 3000 miles on it.

When things are going well, we tend to put blinders on the real issues of life and the real issue that I was having was self-confidence. As I told you earlier on, I relied heavily on others' opinions of me. Towards the end of 2017, our money started acting funny due to poor planning and management. I was worried. The Lord spoke to me and said, "Go visit the Y". Being obedient at that moment was a struggle. Here I am one year later, going back to the place I had moved on from. What will they think? Not only that, I had to dress my almost-two-year-old and take him with me. I looked at the time and knew that if I didn't move then I would regret it. I drove to the city and reached the parking garage just before 10 a.m. I was so happy about that because I only had to pay $20.00 to park for an hour. I went in keeping tabs on the time. Lord knows I didn't want to go over my parking time and end up with a declined payment due to insufficient funds in the bank. I was down to about $40.00 and if I hadn't told you in this story, you would never have known it. Little did I know that I would end up having a conversation with the Early Childhood Director that led me to get a part-time position. It worked out and I owe thanks to a dear friend that encouraged me to talk with the director at the time.

I left that day feeling secure and grateful to God that he yet made a way for me and my family. By 2018 I was working a few days a week, taking care of my family, and doing great in school. I went for my annual physical and boom they labeled me morbidly obese at 283.00 lbs. with an A1c level of 7.3. I went to work on my health I was determined to lose weight, but not before I cried out to the Lord. I wept. Fighting the thoughts in my head once again that said this is your life and there is nothing you can do about it. I drank apple cider vinegar, honey, and warm water each morning before working out. There were days I literally cried as I walked on the treadmill, only to lose 20 lbs.

(By the way 20 lbs. is a big deal). I was so discouraged and went back to eating unhealthily. I tried to mask it by doing things for myself like getting my hair done bi-weekly. My shortcut hairstyle was the bomb! You could not tell me anything. All to make myself feel great and not face the real issue. I dove into schoolwork, taking care of the house, and ministry. There I was again going through the motions of life just existing but not living. Not aware of who I was and whose I was. Doubting myself and continuing to place a burden back in my life that the Lord had lifted self-doubt. Self-doubt is a heavyweight to bear, coupled with fear and you can find yourself in a similar situation.

I needed a haircut, so I reached out to my friend and sis who is a licensed beautician. She got me right and introduced me to detox tea. I was skeptical in the beginning as she talked to me about all the benefits of the detox tea. She described all the symptoms I was having fatigued, not focused, sugar cravings, bloated, constipated, and the list went on. She said, "I am going to give you this two-week supply and I'll follow up with you." I took the packets and made the tea and she followed up with me like she said she would. Well, I felt great! I was no longer bloated; my energy was amazing and my workouts at the gym had improved. Are you ready for the challenge? For me to continue to see improvements in this new weight loss journey I would have to spend some money and I did. I ordered products when I could and when I couldn't I made do with what I had. The weight began to drop off slowly and I became more consistent with creating healthy habits over time. I am now 100 lbs. down and 3 ½ years into my journey. I have had many highs and lows, yet I persevere.

The most important lesson that I have learned, and I hope that I was able to convey through my story is the importance of embracing oneself. Sometimes embracing oneself means to disconnect from the world and really be with yourself. To take your superhero cape off and come to the rescue for yourself, pour into yourself because a depleted vessel cannot serve its purpose. The journey to knowing who you are and whose you are is a lifelong journey. I am so glad that the Lord said "awake from your slumber daughter" I have a plan and a place for you in the kingdom. You are to build up, encourage, and inspire many.

I am truly grateful for my husband and my family that supports me in all my endeavors. When I began to see myself in the eyes of God, my whole world shifted. I look forward to spending time with him. There in his presence, I pour out my heart and he reveals my identity and loves me the same to help me grow and glow. When you begin to grow and glow, God's connections happen. I am grateful for my Destiny helpers. These are individuals that come alongside you to aid you in getting to the place that God wants you to be. It is a sacred place that requires relationships. These individuals can come for a season, a reason, or a lifetime. I will continue to serve in the capacity that God has given me, remembering to pour into myself, saying no when needed, and balancing life along the way in partnership with the best orchestrator God.

Some scriptures that help me throughout my journey to rescue myself are:

Philippians 4:13

I can do all things through Christ which strengtheneth me.

Psalm 120:1

In my distress I cried unto the LORD, and he heard me.

Proverbs 3:6

In all thy ways acknowledge him, and he shall direct thy paths.

Proverbs 16:9

A man's heart deviseth his way: But the LORD directeth his steps.

About
Tamekia Victory

Tamekia Victory is a mother, wife, teacher and Total Life Changes Life Changer. She has over 20 years of teaching experience in Early Childhood education. Tamekia readily shares her passion to inspire and encourage others to be all that God intended them to be, in fact, Tamekia's "Why" is to inspire individuals to deepen their self-awareness so that all people can fulfill their unique life's purpose.

Tamekia has most recently embarked on a new journey to better her health with several lifestyle changes. She is an IBO with Total Life changes and has used this business adventure to launch "Juicing with Victory". Tamekia loves connecting with her customers and coming up with natural ways to encourage healthier choices. She started a Facebook group to encourage some of her family, friends, and followers to MOVE (their bodies) as an entryway to better health.

When it comes down to intuition Tamekia has a natural gift, which is why she has taught young children for over 20 years. She most recently put together her first "Look in a Book" book drive. She collaborated with educators, mothers, friends, and her community to give away new and gently used books for children ages 2-12 years old.

Tamekia is a believer and follower of Jesus Christ. She serves in her church faithfully as a videographer, deaconess, and choir member. Through her church upbringing and training, Tamekia has been able to inspire and encourage. Tamekia is determined to acknowledge God in all her ways, and she is doing just that.

Tamekia is just getting started and she is ready to impact the world. Stay tuned for more...she is on the MOVE! #Takethecapeofsis

If you would like to connect with me or if you would like to learn more about my products and services, please connect with me via email tamekia.victory@gmail.com social media

https://www.facebook.com/tamekia.victory
https://www.instagram.com/meka512/?hl=en
or check out my webpage http://royalvictorys.com/

The Journey Of Me in Pieces
By Tina Marie Bethea-Rodriguez

Hi, I am Tina Marie Bethea-Rodriguez. I arrived in this beautiful world at a very challenging and chaotic time. The time was civil rights. I arrived four days after Dr. Martin Luther King was assassinated. I was born a mulatto baby to Charles and Cathy Bethea.

It was especially difficult for my family. I come from a very diverse background and this set the foundation as I was growing up to see the prejudices and divisions that destroy families and communities because individuals did not understand or see with the eyes of our hearts.

It set me on a road, to put my super cape on for every person who did not have a voice and who was being degraded. I knew what it felt like because it was happening to me at school and with so-called friends, and truth be told, even family members. I would often say I am nothing. Why do they hate me? It was a very difficult period of time for me.

Ladies, did you ever feel unworthy, not good enough, or even loved by anyone? I am very vulnerable to unlocking the keys of that prison for another young girl, lady, or older woman. Let me say from my heart to yours: You are a masterpiece who is worthy of love and every good thing in this world. You have a purpose even though you may not know it now!

My story begins on April 15 in the best borough in the world. The best borough in the world is Brooklyn.

I was born to Charles and Catherine. I weighed 2lbs. I am God's miracle. I began with my mother, Cathy, my relationship with my mother was strangled by the pressures she had from her family and society at best. And she was a young woman who had her own dreams and goals and didn't want a traditional lifestyle. My mom was a working mother which was frowned upon in society back then even as it is today, even though it's not spoken.

My mom was facing many stresses as a woman. As I was later told by my grandmother (her Mom), my mother came home from work one day and packed a bag. I innocently asked mom, "Where is my bag? She looked at me and said, "You are not going!" My little heart shattered into millions of pieces. My heart stopped beating. I couldn't breathe. I screamed. Mommy, please take me. Why don't you love me? I will be good.

That day was April 30, 1972. My mom left to begin a new life without me. I remember my grandma (mom) cradled me in her arms and said you're my baby girl. It will be okay. My grandmother and grandfather raised me to be the woman who stands humbly with the grace of God before you whole, joyful, and grateful.

I held onto bitterness and tried to please people just to be accepted, but as I grew older, I walked the lessons of my mother and other women who walked before us. I saw heartbreak, health issues, voices that couldn't speak.

I saw the power of forgiveness, vulnerability, and strength. To release the part of your past, remember that we are all doing the best we can at any given moment. If we had known that the action would cause pain to others or ourselves, we wouldn't have done it. Retain the lesson and release everything else.

I took my cape off on August 2, 2020. It was the day my mother died from bone cancer, and then two years later I was diagnosed with cancer.

My quote is:
Life will work for me when I realize trouble comes to pass not stay!
And I can do all things through Christ who strengthens me.

Somehow, in the midst of what seems to be the worst possible thing that could happen, you must find the strength that you need to persevere. You must develop the courage that will be required to take the next step. Each individual must face the challenge eyeball to eyeball in order to realize that the challenge comes to make you not break you. Losing a job, home, loved one can be a devastating experience. You can be faced with an unexpected change like a divorce or terminal illness. Whatever your challenge may be, it can rock you to the core. Somehow we must remember that each of us is up for the task.

Remember you have the strength, trust in life to give you the courage that is required to do anything or face anything. As painful or frightening as the difficulty may be, you will do what needs to be done because you have no other choice. Giving up is not an option!

Take a moment to breathe. Allow everything that you are feeling and thinking to move through your body. The moment that you feel that you can't take it or won't make it, reach down into the very core of your being. Damn it, pull a scream out of the very depth of you. Hold onto your power, strength, and the divinity of life within.

Here are three things to state to yourself when adversity strikes:

1. This is going to make me stronger
2. This is going to make me wiser
3. This is going to make me a better person

This challenge, no matter what it is, has come to make you bigger, brighter, stronger, more loving, and compassionate. "IT WILL NOT BREAK YOU"

Until today, you may have been feeling as if you were about to break down. Just for today, call forth the strength, courage, wisdom, insight, power, and love of the spirit of life. Ask that you be guided through the next minute, hour, or day to a place of peace.

Today, I am devoted to calling forth whatever I need to make it through challenging experiences. Are you ready to stand up for your place in life?

About
Tinamarie Rodriguez

Tinamarie Rodriguez is a heart-led leadership speaker and wisdom coach. She teaches empowerment systems that build human connections in individuals' professional and personal lives. Since 1998, Tinamarie Rodriguez has proudly served her community in many capacities.

She is a national expert in the field of self-empowerment and leadership development.

Tinamarie is a beacon of hope traveling the world sharing her "Life is a gift" brand teaching personal and professional systems that build human connections.

Tinamarie demonstrates a history of overcoming some of life's most difficult challenges through persistency, consistency and enduring faith in the human spirit.

Since 1991, Tinamarie has created communication-based curriculums and signature programs for conference-goers and attendees helping meeting planners achieve desired outcomes and learning objectives.

She has acted as a trusted advisor to some of the most prestigious servant leaders in the business community. Her compassionate and patient style allows attendees to visualize goals, take charge of their objectives and follow a customized roadmap to a successful destination.

Serving as CEO of Ms.Tinamarie Speaks LLC, she is a seasoned entrepreneurs and her career endeavors range from being a crisis intervention paraprofessional, special education teacher, a sergeant in the NYPD auxiliary police officer, community liaison for Office of Emergency Management and New York Fema 1 Cert, Facilitator for Ready New York Kids, Immigration paralegal, academic director, and counselor special needs children and adults.

Tinamarie Rodriguez has worked with some of the most successful corporations throughout the United States and abroad.

A Body Called to Rest the Cape
by Aimra'at Allah з Alaliha

For so long I didn't understand the concept of taking care of myself in order to take care of others. I've been full throttle most of my life, giving love to, showing love for, and loving on others.

The love I have exuded is a mere reflection of the love I have been given and taught by my parents and family. For us, loving is like blinking an eye or breathing. Loving is a very natural thing for me to do, and it has been a superpower I have used generously. My capacity to love has caused me to give emotionally and spiritually even when physically, I was so tapped out that I shouldn't have. Though, how do you say no to love? How do you say no to the power of healing when the remedy is as simple as love? When as a Mother, Daughter, Sister, Friend, Lover, a Wife - as a Woman there is so much to be healed, cared for, and protected? This had been my thinking, my motivation most of my life. I know now that I've been wearing a cape longer than I can ever recall.

I have countless accounts of being there for people. From the times I stepped in to physically fight as a young girl and into my teens; as a peer counselor in high school when I sat in a bungalow for an entire class period available to other students in distress who otherwise had no other outlet or opportunity to release; the battles I fought as a mother for the security, safety, and protection of my child's well-being; or as a partner and wife loving in spite of and giving without a fair return while carrying loads.

Though, I'll tell you about a season in my life when I believed it most necessary to keep the cape on, and boy was I wrong! In November 2011, two days before my 36th birthday, I was diagnosed with Cervical Cancer. It was removed by the end of that month, and as I lay healing at home in December with the time to figure out my life and next moves, I was convinced that the true work of my calling was serving God's people through ministry in the church, the community, and however I could through my business while simultaneously building and promoting it.

As I said before, I was convinced of what must be done and how to make it happen! Also determined to show up as a powerful survivor whose life had been spared of a ravaging disease that I had watched and known to have taken the lives of family and countless loved ones. This determination pushed me through school to complete programs I had left undone, to get my certifications and degrees. In combining my knowledge and experience, I developed programs and curriculum for the next generations to grow from and to live freely. Programs and circles for women and parents in which for each person I became a breakthrough partner. I willingly and lovingly had sleepless nights and gave hours to fasting and prayer all to see the miraculous. And I did!

And this was not half of it, the business I was building at the time was actually two businesses. My gift of sewing was taking off, and I was busy with pop-up shops to showcase my creations and clientele was building from my one-of-a-kind designs. Another business grew out of the gift of administration and customer service. This business I was able to incorporate into ministry. My event planning, coordinating, and hosting gave me the opportunities to expose people to ministry events and share the goodness of what was happening within the four walls of the church and gather like spirits! The work was indeed purposeful and again miracles were happening and healing was taking place.

There was no stopping me determined as I was! At my church home, I preached on assignment and taught the youth weekly. I preached, conducted workshops, engaged in panel discussions, and led seminars within my church home and as a guest in others. As a leader of the National Cervical Cancer Coalition, I spoke at numerous events and gatherings teaching facts, prevention, and sharing my story as a survivor and the impact that my spirituality had on my healing process.

I worked as a Community Organizer for the great City of Los Angeles, standing on the front lines for the betterment of the people in the city's communities. I connected with affiliate organizations and churches for more ministry opportunities and exposure. And I began using my skills and certificates in Chemical Dependency to serve the youth at facilities I also connected with as an organizer. It was, as I was convinced, a grand time of purposeful work. I ultimately took my work to the LA County Department of Mental Health to jumpstart my Clinical Psychology path and be of even greater service.

And with all that busyness my cape had not yet weighed me down enough to take it off. Yet it was the matters closest to my heart that made me feel the weight. While I was clinging to relationships, some needing to end and others just needing to grow up. I was dealing with how my heart was feeling while watching my only child get ready to leave home for college. This forced me to get ready to enter the "Empty Nest Syndrome" well before her actual departure. It was a hurtful and emotional space I lived in for years and quite bittersweet because there were so many great things celebrated with my daughter, her accomplishments, and successful endeavors. There were moments I can't even count to this day of my laughter and pride, turning into tears of sadness and what was to come. I was witnessing the very thing that brought me pure joy and unconditional love be excited to go for the start of a life of her own separate from me.

The cape was getting heavier, yet I was still loving, and I was still convinced and determined to push through. Have you ever been in survival mode? Just "going through the motions" of life? You see, you don't have to have had a life-threatening disease or be close to death and still be alive to be a survivor. ***BECAUSE YOU ARE ALIVE AND READING THIS YOU ARE A SURVIVOR!*** We are all surviving this thing called life, going through in different ways and our push through based on what we have convinced ourselves of is what makes how we show up to the world look different for each of us.

My purpose in sharing my story with you is to show you another way to survive and to impart another option for you to take that's worthy of you taking your cape off! My story is to remind you that the superpower of Love, specifically Love for self, is what will save you, and take you out of survival mode. Allow yourself to see the strength and power in caring for You. Bottom line. Love you more than you love anyone else.

My cape stayed on through taking my daughter to college and returning home alone to broken relationships and a life of busyness. Instead of taking off the heavy cape, seeing who I was in that moment, dealing with my pains, disappointments, and decisions I made that caused me to sit in seats I was comfortable in, and take blame and accountability for my own life - I kept saving others, healing others, and loving others instead of loving myself; instead of saving me and healing myself to wholeness. This only led to another broken relationship and marriage and ultimately another divorce.

It took for me having a stroke to realize how important it was for me to love and take care of myself first, in order for me to care for and love anyone else. In November 2019, on a Friday, 5 days before my 46th birthday, I suffered multiple strokes that began in my sleep, continued onto the next day, and didn't stop until I made it to the emergency room late Saturday afternoon. Prior to the stroke, I knew that having cancer, suffering from migraines, and a few other things that were going on with my body were all red flags of not taking care of myself and making some deep life changes. I knew I needed to love myself more than I loved anyone else. While still feeling the vibrations of the stroke in my body sitting in the triage unit, I said to God, "Okay whatever this is, it can't take too long because I have things to do. I got it." The next thing I knew, it was about brunch time on Sunday, and I was waking up to familiar faces! It was being restricted and having no choice to let people take care of me for everything. That made me see how much I really needed the care. It was the looks on the face of my brother and my daughter as they stayed by my bedside day and night, sleeping in uncomfortable positions to not miss a beat with me that opened my eyes to how delicate and vulnerable I was and how loved I am. And all of THAT convinced me that I deserved to use my own superpower of Love on myself. It was time to be determined to love myself more and more than anyone else first!

By the time I was discharged, with a walker and a plan of care, I realized that it was time to take the cape off and wrap myself in it. The stroke spoke from within and showed me how tired I was. That I was exhausted, and that I would have to **overstand** the true nature of my calling and the work I was purposed to do, and that it could only be done if I was well enough to do so holistically. I had to learn that my cup would have to be full in order for me to pour into others, and it's even better when my cup is overflowing.

Today I continue to serve, and I do so from a cup overflowing with Love. Overflowing because I have learned and continuously practice Self-Love and Self-Care consistently-no matter what and no matter who-this is me pouring into myself. I willingly and lovingly keep my cape on throughout the week because I may be called to serve at any given moment and in many ways, so I intentionally take my cape off every Sunday. That is my day to do nothing I don't want to do and only what I want to do; it is "My Self-Care Day," 100% me day!

Since taking the cape off, my expressions of love may be experienced in all that I do whether personal or business. I combine my knowledge, skills, experiences, with my lifestyle changes for better health, and I incorporate a holistic modality into my work. As a Healer and Alchemist, I aid by using herbs and a number of essential oils that soothe, calm, and even protect and clear the Mind, Body, and Spirit from negative energies, the elements, and many ailments from my product-based business; products that serve the entire family. And my service-based business offers packages that support and serve the Entrepreneur, Visionary, and Businesses on all levels.

My hope for you is encouragement and strength from my story. If you have not before today, choose now to take your cape off and use it to cover yourself with your own love, your own healing, and to power up yourself. And choose at least one day to **DO NOTHING EXCEPT POUR LOVE INTO YOU... BECAUSE YOU SO DESERVE IT!**

"When it's all love, there's no danger. Nothing to be cautious or afraid of. Bring back the love, let it save us. So we can be one with no danger." Rahsaan Patterson

About
Aimra'at Allah و Alaliha,
Formerly "Rasha Ellen Patterson"

Aimra'at Allah و Alaliha, formerly Rasha Ellen Patterson, is from the Bronx, New York, born November 6, 1975 to Native New Yorkers and raised in the best of both worlds between New York and California. Aimra'at is a survivor; she survived sexual abuse, verbal and emotional abuse as a little girl, she has survived the loss of a child, in her late 20's she survived domestic violence, she is cancer free surviving Cervical Cancer for 11 years and counting, and she is surviving and thriving after a stroke in 2019. Called to serve, Aimra'at has done so willingly in many ways; as an ordained preacher she has taught and worked as an administrator to leadership, while establishing and actively building youth mentorship programs and women groups; with a passion for Psychology, she focused on Chemical Dependency and Abnormal Behavior, working in group homes, clinics, schools, and in her communities; always taking opportunities and the advantage of many platforms to serve. Additionally, Aimra'at is an Administrator and Customer Service Professional and has been serving as such for 29 years in various industries.

Continuing to serve today, Aimra'at combines her knowledge, skills, experiences, and her lifestyle changes for better health in all that she does and has incorporated a holistic modality into her work, as well, the products and services she provides. She has a product-based business, "In Love, Aimra'at" which offers products to enhance the person and the home. And from her service-based business, "Professional Results" (PR), she provides service packages that help with daily tasks and operations for a business of any size; She trains on the topic "The Gift of Service and the Key Elements of Customer Service", teaching customer service teams how to provide exceptional service, how to create amazing customer and client experiences, how to build relationships with your clients, and how to understand clients as value to your business and to your company's bottom line. She successfully improves employee relationships by increasing the culture around offering great service on all levels. Catering to visionaries and entrepreneurs, Professional Results, offers support packages, subscriptions, and opportunities to grow and connect at a PR networking mixer or entrepreneurial workshop, and at a PR Pop-Up Shop where entrepreneurs are able to promote, build, and expand their business.

Aimra'at has the ability to connect and transform. And she enjoys networking and genuinely connecting with people to get to know them, to understand how she may be of service, and build amazing relationships and partnerships.

Aimra'at Allah و Alaliha is a coach, author (Rasha Patterson) and speaks on Survivorship, Healing, and Transitioning In Life. Aimra'at is a student of Alchemy and a practicing Alchemist. She is in "the service of healing" and offers herself as a Breakthrough Partner.

Pronunciations:
Aimra'at:
EYEMRAH-OTT Allah:
Alluh و: MWA
Alaliha: AA-LUH-LEE-HAH
Affectionately "Roxy"